JOHN CONSTABLE

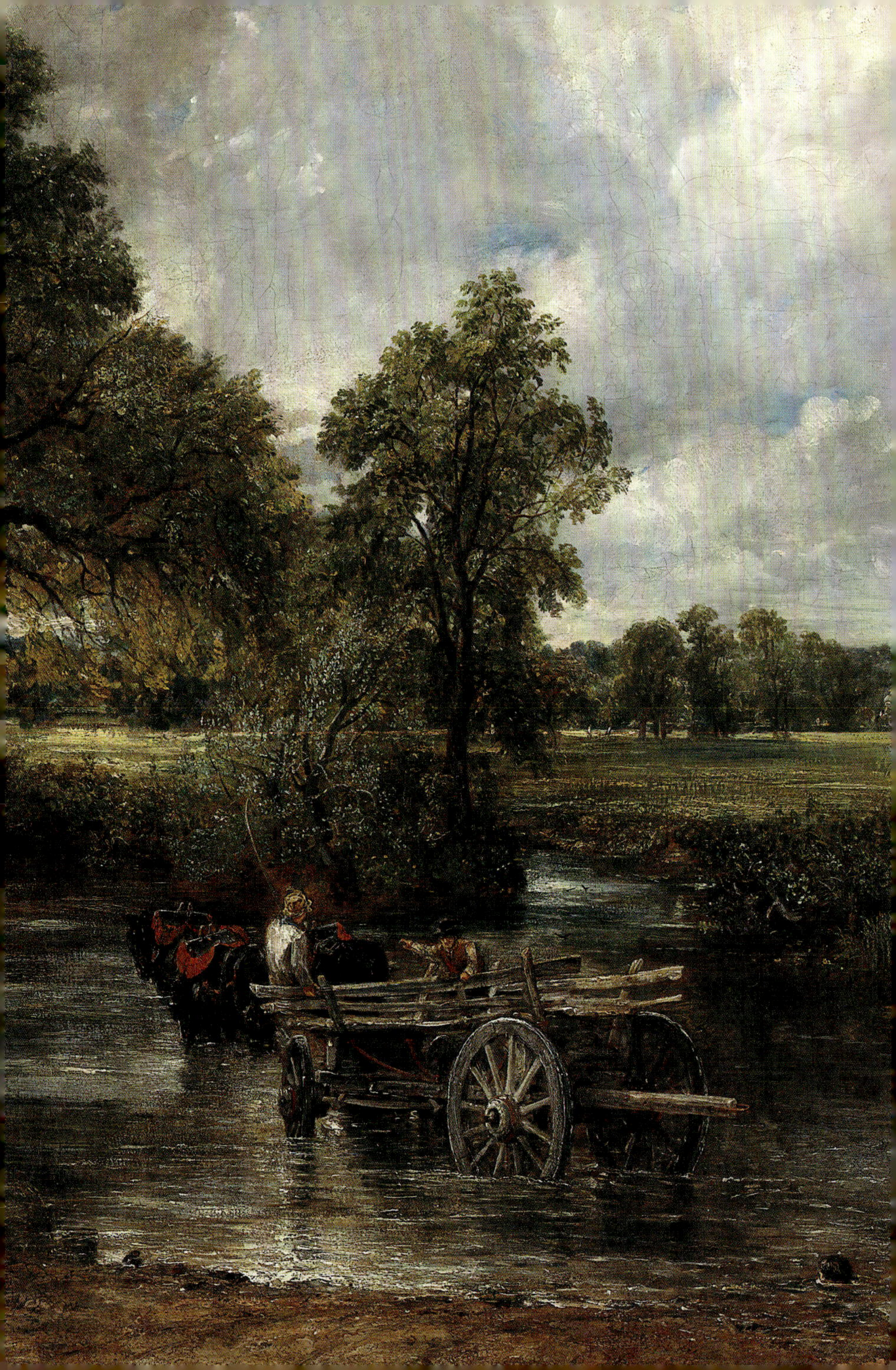

JOHN CONSTABLE

GILLIAN FORRESTER

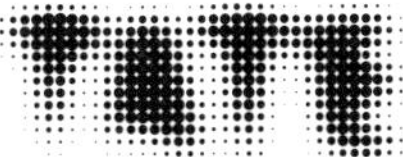

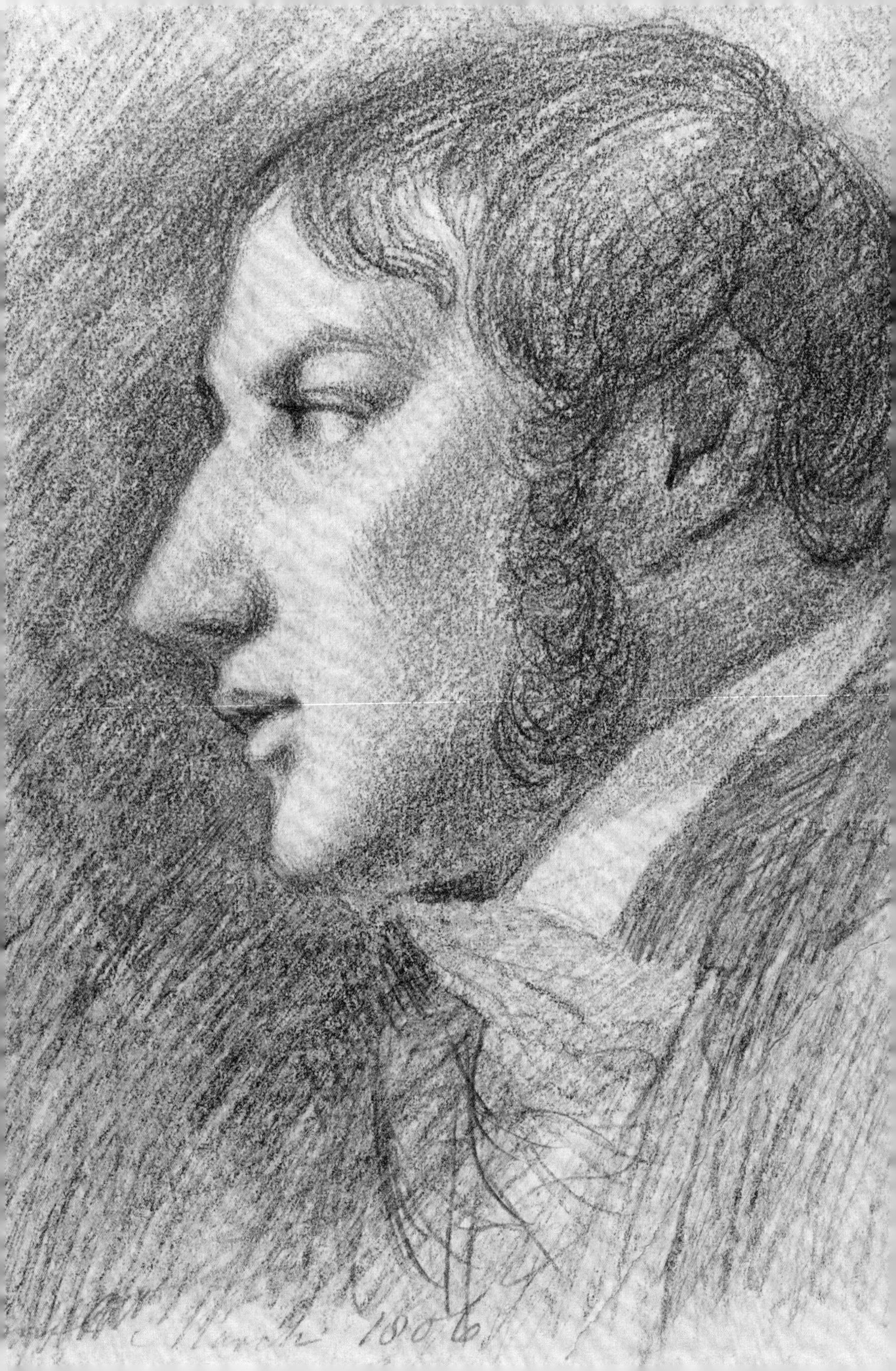

1806

John Constable is one of the most celebrated British artists, his fame only equalled by that of his contemporary and rival, J.M.W. Turner. *The Hay Wain* 1820–1 (pp.2 [detail], 22), the painting he exhibited at the Royal Academy in 1821, is a familiar icon; reproduced on posters, jigsaws, biscuit tins and other household objects, this ubiquitous image embodies a nostalgic fantasy of nineteenth-century English rural life that still resonates powerfully in the post-industrial, post-agrarian society of the twenty-first century. Yet during his lifetime, even in his native country, Constable's work failed to receive the universal acclaim that he craved. He was critiqued and ridiculed in the press and by his peers for his unconventional handling of paint and audacious use of colour. Constable responded to his critics with defiance and conviction, but died feeling bitter and misunderstood. The penetrating self-portrait Constable drew in 1806, when he was thirty (opposite), conveys something of the complexity and seriousness of this often troubled artist.

This short book maps Constable's arduous and remarkable trajectory from his childhood and adolescence in rural Suffolk to his death in London at the age of sixty in 1837, a truncated career that nonetheless resulted in an immense body of work – paintings, drawings, sketchbooks and prints – now dispersed in museums and private collections around the world. Constable was also a prolific letter writer and a substantial trove of correspondence with family, friends and patrons has survived, providing rich insights into his intertwined artistic, intellectual and private lives. This correspondence was the basis for the first biography of Constable, written by his close friend and fellow artist Charles Robert Leslie and published in 1843, which remains a rich, insightful portrait of the artist.[1]

Detail of *The Hay Wain*
1820–1, exh.1821
Oil paint on canvas
130.2 × 185.4
See p.22

Self-portrait, March 1806
1806
Graphite on paper
19 × 14.5

Constable was born in the village of East Bergholt in the county of Suffolk on 11 June 1776. His father, Golding Constable, was a prosperous mill-owner, grain and coal merchant and gentleman farmer who had married Ann Watts, the daughter of a wealthy London barrel manufacturer, in 1767. Although Golding is often described as a miller, he was in fact a formidable entrepreneur with extensive mercantile interests, and John and his two brothers and three sisters had a comfortable upbringing at East Bergholt House. The Constables were considered middle class, but had connections with wealthy families and the local gentry that were to facilitate John's career. He showed a talent for drawing and nurtured ambitions to become an artist but, in a society preoccupied with class and status, artists were typically regarded as little more than artisans. Constable's parents certainly considered the profession to be too precarious and of dubious social status; it was decided that while his older brother, also named Golding, would take over the family business, John would be ordained as a priest in the Church of England.

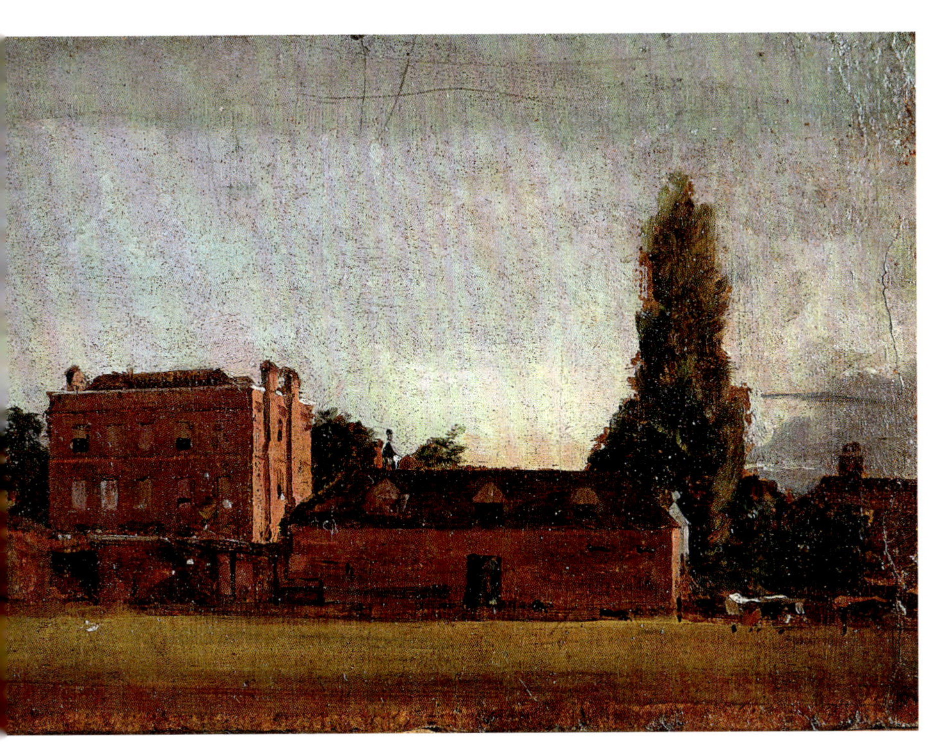

East Bergholt House c.1811
Oil paint on board on panel
182 × 502

As the younger Golding grew up, however, it became clear that he had a learning disability, and John was forced to join the firm after he left grammar school at the age of sixteen. His initial duties were generally practical rather than managerial, and included working in a windmill, observing meteorological conditions and familiarising himself with the Stour, the busy river on which the family's fleet of barges travelled to transport flour, coal and other commodities. Constable was unenthusiastic about transitioning to a managerial role; he continued to draw and was taught the rudiments of painting by John Dunthorne, a local plumber and glazier who was also an accomplished amateur artist. He also spent time in London and had informal teaching there from two artists, John Cranch and John Thomas Smith, who also encouraged him to build a collection of books and prints. When his younger brother Abram joined the family firm in 1799, Constable was released to study at the Royal Academy Schools in London.

The seven years Constable spent working for his father were not wasted. His intimate knowledge of the 'scenes of his careless boyhood', as he later put it – the mills, locks, towpaths, cornfields and woods – provided him with a rich trove of raw material for his art. The Suffolk landscape, he declared, 'made me a painter'.[2] Although his career choice necessitated moving to London, Constable continued to visit Suffolk regularly while he was a student, compulsively drawing and painting outdoors. In the autumn of 1802 his father, now more supportive, bought him a studio in Dedham, two miles from East Bergholt, and while Constable continued to rent lodgings in London and exhibited at the Royal Academy, he did not settle in the metropolis until he married in 1816. The physical, social and emotional landscape of his native Suffolk remained a lifelong preoccupation, and the area is often described today as 'Constable country' – a moniker that it acquired even during the artist's lifetime.

ROYAL ACADEMY STUDENT

At the Royal Academy, young men were admitted first as probationers to draw from casts in the Antique School. They were required to submit a proficient drawing to become full students, and would continue to draw casts until they were considered ready to graduate to the Life School. Constable became a probationer in March 1799 and a full student in June 1800. He attended the life academy diligently for many years, making drawings and paintings, including a life-drawing that likely depicts the well-known model Samuel Strowger, a former farm-worker from Suffolk whom Constable already knew (opposite). Full students were also allowed to use the Royal Academy Library, and attend lectures and exhibitions. Painting was not formally taught, however, and students relied on swapping tips with their peers, receiving informal tuition from experienced artists and observing 'Varnishing Days' at the Royal Academy's annual exhibition, when painters were permitted to make final alterations after their canvases had been hung.

Constable was some ten years older than the majority of his classmates: Turner, for instance, who was a just a year older than Constable, had become a probationer in 1789 and was elected an Associate Royal Academician in 1799, Constable's probationary year. Acutely aware of his junior status, Constable swiftly acquired a reputation for being sensitive to criticism and perceived slights, and made few friends among his fellow students. Some of the most successful artists of the

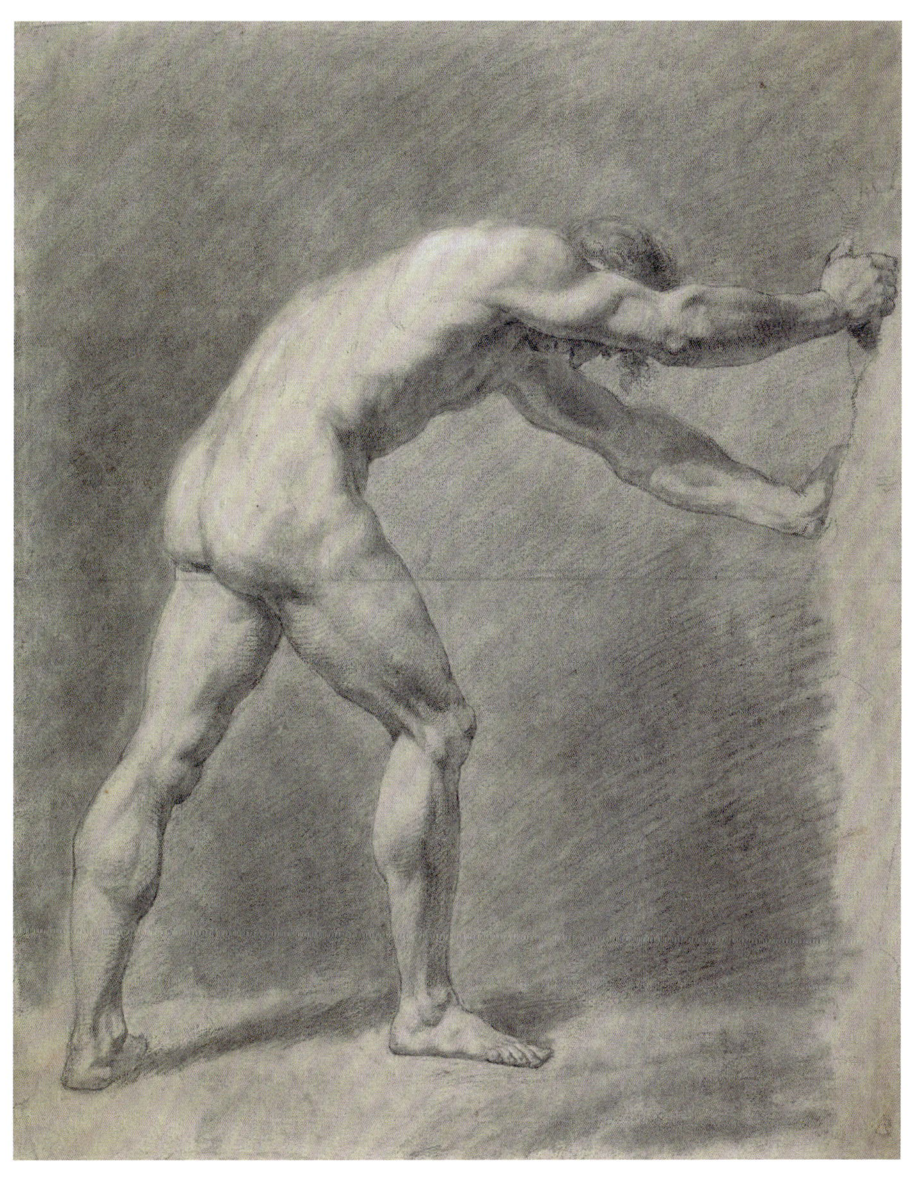

Male Nude 1808
Graphite and gouache
on paper
55.2 × 44.5

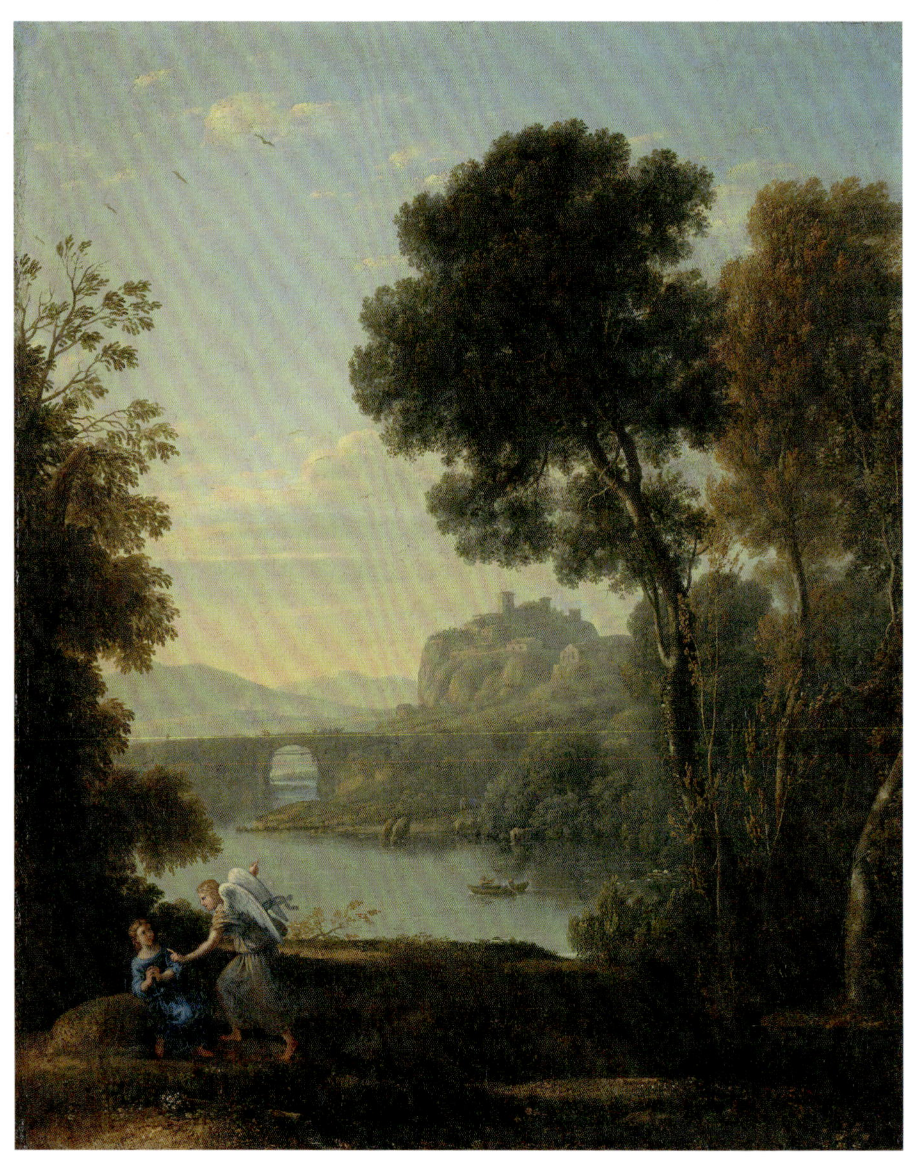

Claude Lorrain
*Landscape with Hagar
and the Angel* 1646
Oil paint on canvas
mounted on wood
52.2 × 42.3

period, including Turner and Sir Thomas Lawrence,
came from working-class origins, whereas Constable, who
was bankrolled by his father, was regarded as a dilettante
rather than professional artist, a reputation he worked hard
to counteract. His friends were typically older figures who
acted as mentors, such as the wealthy collector and amateur
artist Sir George Beaumont and the influential landscape
painter and Royal Academician Joseph Farington, or younger
men with whom he felt an affinity, among them the American
painter C.R. Leslie and the Anglican cleric the younger
John Fisher.

Like his fellow students, Constable supplemented his
education at the Royal Academy by viewing the work of
other artists, both contemporary and historical. The British
Museum was the only public museum in London at that period,
and admission was restricted, but from 1808 Royal Academy
students were able to view the antique sculptures gifted by
Charles Townley as well as the prints and drawings collection.
There were also commercial exhibitions and viewings at
auction houses, and well-connected students could access
private collections. Seventeenth-century classical or 'historical'
landscape by European artists such as Claude Lorrain and
Nicolas Poussin was revered in Britain at the period, in
preference to indigenous landscape by contemporary artists.
In the *Discourses*, the inaugural lecture series he gave between
1769 and 1790, Sir Joshua Reynolds, the first president of the
Royal Academy, laid out a hierarchy of artistic categories,
privileging history painting, the representation of important
events from classical mythology, ancient history or the
Bible. Landscape was considered inferior, and portraiture
even lowlier. (Ironically, Reynolds himself made his living
from painting society portraits, finding his history paintings
difficult to sell.) In 1795, Constable had met Sir George
Beaumont, whose mother lived in Dedham; Beaumont owned
several outstanding works by the French seventeenth-century
painter Claude Lorrain, notably *Landscape with Hagar and the
Angel* 1646 (opposite), an exquisite, atmospheric picture
that Beaumont famously carried with him on his travels in
a specially made case. Constable admired Claude's idealised,
formulaic work immensely, but did not share Beaumont's
conservative insistence that modern works should merely
imitate those of the old masters.

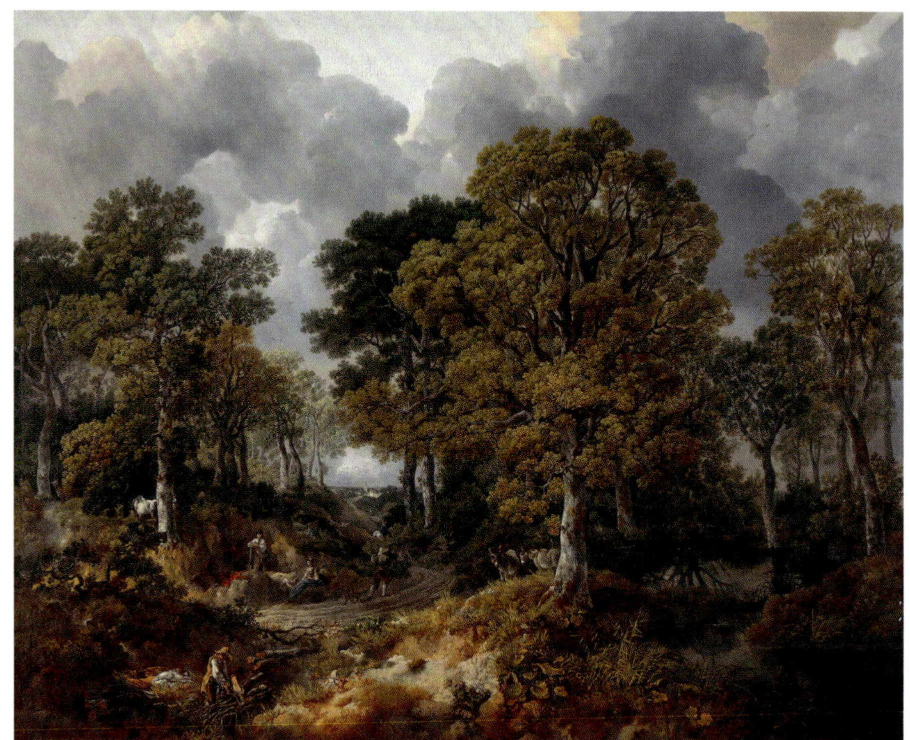

THE NATURAL PAINTER

Thomas Gainsborough
*Cornard Wood, near Sudbury,
Suffolk* 1748
Oil paint on canvas
122 × 155

In April 1802, Constable exhibited for the first time in the Royal Academy annual exhibition. Farington noted that the painting he showed – which cannot now be conclusively identified – had 'a great of merit but is rather too cold', and advised that Constable 'study nature & *particular* art less'.[3] After visiting Beaumont the following month, Constable wrote a lengthy letter to his friend John Dunthorne in which he revealed his commitment to making art that was distinctive and personal:

> For the last two years I have been running after pictures, and seeking the truth at second hand. I have not endeavoured to represent nature with the same elevation of mind with which I set out, but have rather tried to make my performances look like the work of other men… I shall return to Bergholt, where I shall endeavour to get a pure and unaffected manner of representing the scenes that may employ me. There is little or nothing in the exhibition

worth looking up to. There is room enough for a natural painture [sic].[4]

The search for a 'natural painture' would preoccupy Constable for the rest of his career. That summer he retreated to Suffolk, where he painted his first canvas of Dedham Vale (p.34). The composition clearly references Beaumont's *Landscape with Hagar and the Angel* (p.10), yet Constable's choice of a British site with deep personal meaning not only marked his independence from conventional notions of landscape painting but hinted, too, at the radical nature of his vision. He was also familiar with the work of the eighteenth-century British landscape painter Richard Wilson, and was particularly fascinated by Thomas Gainsborough, who was born and raised in Sudbury, just sixteen miles from East Bergholt. Wilson, tragically, died in abject poverty, and Gainsborough made his living from fashionable portraiture even though his avowed true vocation lay with landscape. Constable was familiar with Gainsborough's landscape drawings and paintings; his wealthy uncle, David Pike Watts, owned Gainsborough's early Suffolk masterpiece *Cornard Wood* 1748, which Constable greatly admired (opposite). The lingering influence of Gainsborough was particularly strong in Constable's early landscapes, including his *Woodland Scene overlooking Dedham Vale* (p.35).

PORTRAIT 'JOBBING'

Like Gainsborough, and with greater reluctance, Constable also painted portraits, terming his commissions 'jobs'. Despite their attempts to elevate the genre, portraitists invariably found themselves working under frustrating aesthetic constraints and intense commercial pressures. Running a successful portrait practice demanded a range of skills in addition to the obvious requirement of being able to make a good (or at least flattering) likeness of a sitter, including business acumen, social connections, tact and diplomacy. Golding Constable's network of connections with landowning and mercantile families provided a steady supply of commissions for his son, who painted around one hundred portraits over the course of his career. Traditionally dismissed as inferior to Constable's other works, these have recently risen in critical standing.[5]

Constable settled into a routine of painting portraits of local people in the mornings and focusing on landscape in the afternoons. In 1804 George Bridges, a banker, merchant

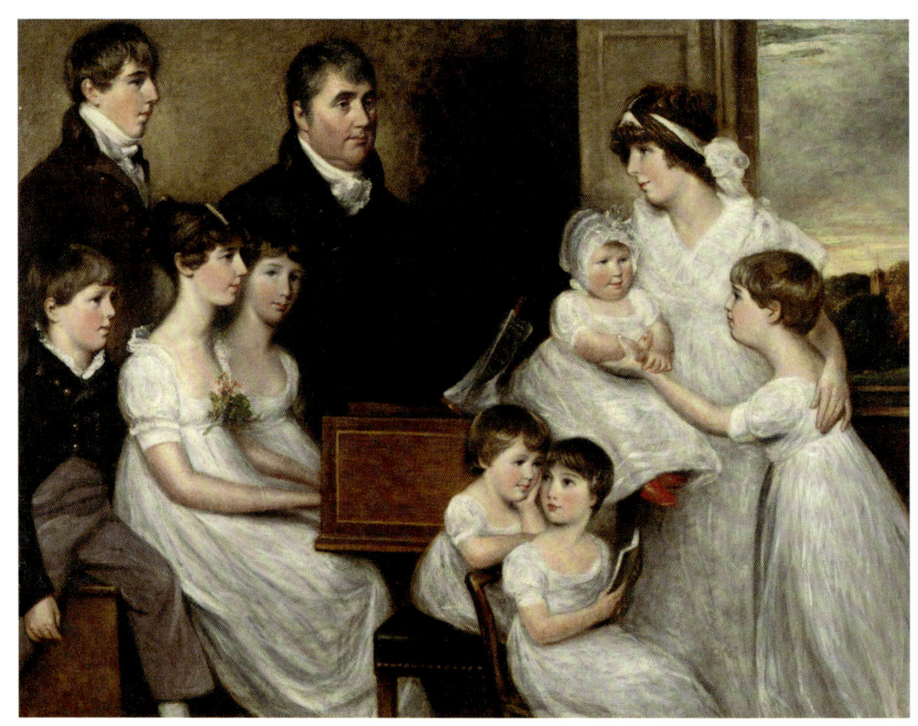

and business associate of Golding Constable's, who lived in
Essex, the county adjacent to Suffolk, commissioned Constable
to paint a portrait of his family (above). This was an ambitious
project for Constable, who typically painted single portraits,
since Bridges and his wife Mary had eight children. Constable
stayed at the Bridges' home, Lawford House, for several weeks.
His practice, which was typical of the period, was to paint
directly onto the canvas without preliminary drawings; if he
did make such drawings of all the family members there, few
have survived. The final work is somewhat awkward, more an
assemblage of individual portraits than a harmonised group
in which the family members appear to interact. Although
Constable went on to paint other group portraits, this was
the most ambitious he ever attempted. He experimented
with different formats, settling on the head-and-shoulders
view typically known as 'three-quarters', and seems to have
preferred working on a modest scale: the awkward portrait
he painted of Rear-Admiral Western in 1813 is his only known
full-length.

The Bridges Family
1804
Oil paint on canvas
135.9 × 183.8

Constable also had several commissions for 'portraits' of country estates. These included Malvern Court near Solihull, where he also painted portraits of the owner Henry Griswold Lewis and his ward Mary Freer (p.37), and Wivenhoe House in Essex, though the latter seems more of a landscape since the house appears as a detail in the background (pp.48–9). He also made numerous drawings and paintings of his own family home, East Bergholt House, for which he had a deep affection (see, for example, pp.6–7).

He continued to work as a portraitist until the late 1820s, using his studio in London after he settled in the city in 1816. His most animated portraits were of his family and close friends: they include the trio of portraits of his fiancée Maria Bicknell, his close friend John Fisher, and Fisher's wife Mary, all of which Constable painted in 1816, the year that both John and Mary Fisher and Constable and Maria married (pp.21, 50, 51).

The previous year, Constable had painted separate portraits of his parents, Golding and Ann Constable, though Golding appears much younger than a man of seventy-six (pp.44, 45). The portraits soon acquired a poignant, commemorative function: Ann died in May 1815, having become unwell when gardening, and Golding died the following year. After his mother's death, in July and August 1815 Constable painted views of his parents' flower and vegetable gardens and the surrounding farmland from the windows of East Bergholt House (pp.46, 47). His mother, significantly, had laid out the flower bed in the year before she died, and the lengthening shadows over the garden seem to evoke her recent death. As Constable was painting these elegiac tributes to his parents, he was surely aware that the traditional way of life at East Bergholt he had always known and cherished was coming to an end in the face of political reform and relentless industrialisation.

THE PICTURESQUE

In 1806 Constable went on a seven-week sketching tour of the Lake District, the generic term for the counties of Cumberland and Westmorland in the north of England. The area was not yet associated in the popular imagination with Romantic writers such as Wordsworth and Coleridge, but was already a destination for artists and tourists due to its promotion by the Reverend William Gilpin, who had developed his theory of the picturesque first in his *Three Essays on the Picturesque* (1792) and subsequently in a series of illustrated travel itineraries. Always a vague concept, the picturesque was defined by Gilpin as 'that peculiar kind of beauty, which is agreeable in a picture', and provided a method for viewing landscape, stressing the aesthetic appeal of roughness and ruination.[6]

Although Gilpin's theory was often derided for being absurdly formulaic, it was influential for a generation of landscape artists that included Turner and his contemporary Thomas Girtin. Constable adhered to the picturesque throughout his career, in a letter of 1834 attributing the 'broken ruggedness of my style' to its ongoing influence.[7] Constable did not find the Lake District congenial, but he made there a remarkable series of graphite drawings and atmospheric watercolours, which he used as raw material for paintings over the next three years (p.36).

The sketching tour was a standard component of the landscape artist's work regime at the period. Turner and Girtin, for example, undertook regular, carefully planned, trips, usually following well-established itineraries (including those devised by Gilpin), to gather raw material for their finished watercolours and paintings made for patrons and for exhibition. They were also commissioned by print publishers to make drawings for engravings which were typically published in serial form. A journey to Italy via France and Switzerland was considered an essential part of an artist's education, but when the wars with Napoleon made travel to continental Europe virtually impossible between 1793 and 1815, artists instead found inspiration in the landscapes of Britain, producing works that celebrated the nation's military and economic strength.

After war ended, many artists flocked to the continent – but not Constable, the constant outlier, who never left England, and after 1806 only travelled in the south of England, preferring to depict sites with which he had a personal emotional connection. In 1821 he wrote to John Fisher: 'I should paint my own places best. Painting is but another word for feeling.'[8] His other close friend, C.R. Leslie, observed that the subjects Constable depicted formed 'a history of his affections'.[9]

One of Constable's 'own places' was Salisbury, in the south-west of England. In 1798 he had met Dr John Fisher, rector of Langham Church in Essex, who, following several promotions, was appointed as Bishop of Salisbury in 1807. A devout Anglican, Constable corresponded regularly with Fisher, and in 1811 spent three weeks staying with the bishop and his wife Dorothea in Salisbury. During his visit, Constable made numerous drawings of the cathedral, including a group in black and white chalks on blue paper (now faded to grey; see p.38), and he also visited other well-known sites in the area, including the ancient hill fort of Old Sarum – a subject to which, like Salisbury Cathedral, he would repeatedly return.

On this first visit he met John Fisher's nephew, also named John, who was working as his uncle's chaplain and was to be ordained the following year. The younger Fisher and Constable immediately became close friends, and their extensive correspondence provides compelling insights into Constable's art, his religious beliefs and his fraught emotional life. Bishop Fisher died in 1826 but Constable continued to visit Salisbury as his nephew had been made canon there in 1819 and later became archdeacon.

'MY NATIVE SCENES'

In 1812, Constable exhibited a painting of Salisbury Cathedral and three Suffolk landscapes at the Royal Academy. One of these was *Summer Evening*, a view of cattle grazing at sunset with the crescent moon visible in the sky, which Constable painted from the garden of his East Bergholt neighbour Sarah Roberts. Constable may have had in mind the celebrated seventeenth-century Flemish painter Peter Paul Rubens's monumental painting of his country estate, Het Stein, known as *The Rainbow Landscape* c.1636, which belonged to Beaumont (p.39). That summer, he wrote in a letter, 'I have succeeded most with my native scenes … I have now very distinctly marked out a path for myself and I am desirous of pursuing it uninterruptedly'.[10] An anonymous critic's comment, however – 'MR CONSTABLE has much originality and vigour of style, but bordering perhaps a little on crudeness of effect' – created consternation at East Bergholt, adding to familial concerns that Constable's work was insufficiently saleable.[11] Constable was also advised by Joseph Farington that 'the objection made to His pictures was their being unfinished', and that he should study Claude Lorrain's paintings to remedy the problem.[12]

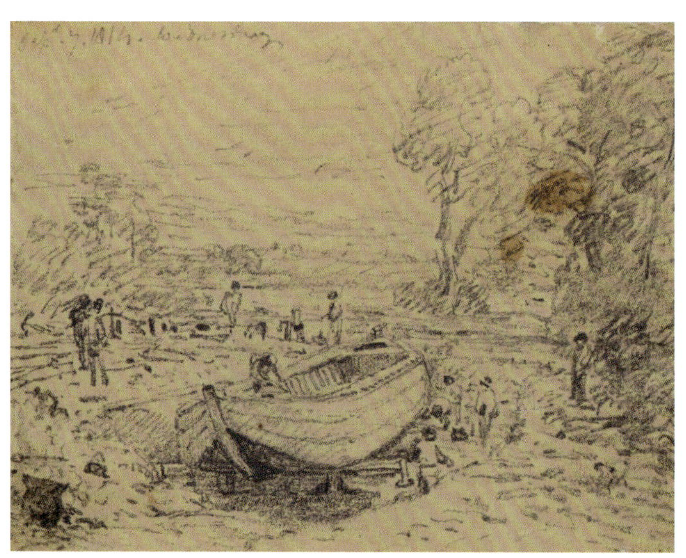

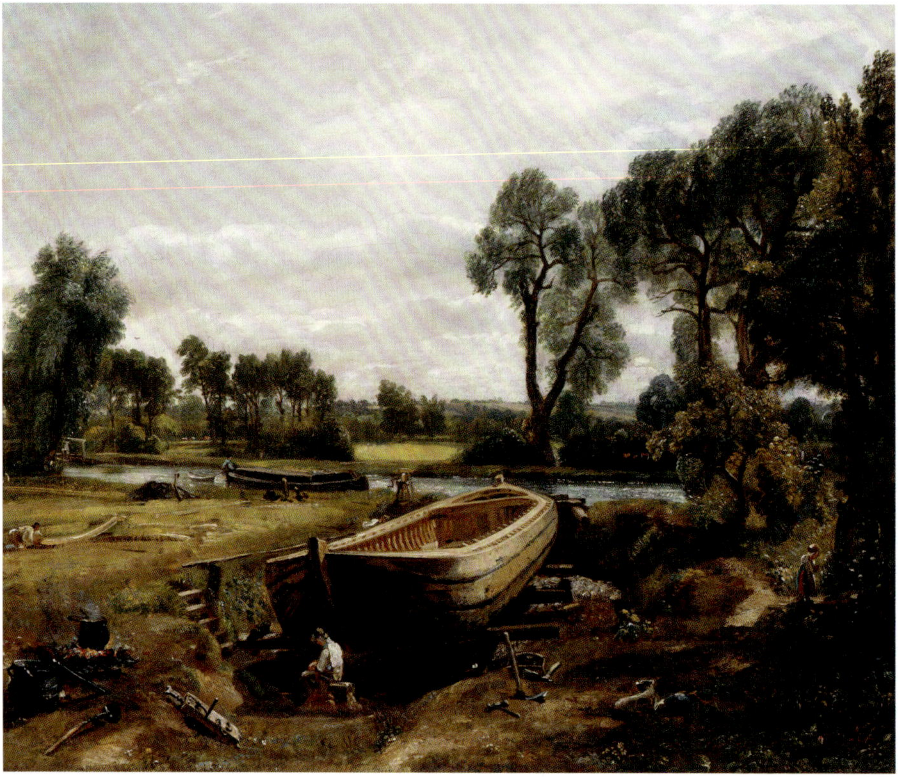

Constable was not the only artist subjected to negative comments regarding his technique and use of colours; the issue seems to have been partly generational, with older artists, collectors and critics who valued smoothness and muted coloration in painting attacking younger, more radical artists. J.M.W. Turner, for example, was routinely scolded for his 'uncouth' handling of paint and for using pale colours to prime or 'ground' his canvases, giving greater luminosity to the image. Beaumont particularly disliked his work. Constable attempted to remedy the supposed deficiency of 'uncouthness' in 1816, when he exhibited the highly finished *The Wheatfield* (in the collection of the Clark Art Institute, Massachusetts), but reverted to his personal and idiosyncratic method of painting, which consisted of priming his canvases with dark colours, and making vigorous use of brushes – and, from 1816, a palette knife – to create a range of marks and textures to replicate both what he saw in nature and the feelings it evoked in him.

Constable was also committed to painting outdoors. This practice was not innovative, as British and European landscape artists had been working en plein air for decades, but Constable was radical in resolving to make all his studies on the spot. In 1815, he exhibited *Boat-Building near Flatford Mill*, which he had painted outdoors the previous autumn, having made a detailed drawing in one of his sketchbooks (opposite). The painting depicts a barge under construction, which would presumably join Golding Constable's fleet. In the same year Constable exhibited *The Stour Valley and Dedham Village* (pp.42–3), which he had been working on concurrently with *Boat-Building* and which he may have also painted completely outdoors. In the background, Constable painted an idyllic panoramic view of the valley, but the foreground is dominated by a massive manure-heap, known locally as a 'dungle', flanked by two labourers in the process of filling their cart. The idea of depicting agricultural toil was not original; it was a popular subject during the Napoleonic Wars, intended to bolster a sense of national identity and self-sufficiency during an economic blockade. Constable would have seen Turner's *Ploughing up Turnips, near Slough* at the Royal Academy in 1809; the painting depicted agricultural labourers gathering turnips, with the distinctive silhouette of Windsor Castle in the background. His decision to foreground his painting

Page from sketchbook used by artist in Essex and Sussex between July and October 1814, 7 September 1814
Graphite on paper
80 × 108

Boat-Building near Flatford Mill
1814–15, exh.1815
Oil paint on canvas
50.8 × 61.6

with a pile of dung was distinctive, however, and signalled his conviction that the lowliest objects were worthy of being painted and displayed on the walls of the Royal Academy.

Constable was striving to create a new language of artmaking during a period of great emotional turbulence. In 1809 he was introduced to Maria Bicknell, whom he had first encountered when she was thirteen (opposite). Maria's grandfather was the Rev. Dr Durand Rhudde, rector of the parish of Brantham-cum-Bergholt, and the encounter took place during one of her visits to her wealthy and formidable relative. Maria's family were unenthusiastic about her relationship with Constable, refusing to accept the artist as their social equal: his chosen profession was considered precarious, even morally questionable; moreover, he was eleven years older than Maria, a significant age difference even for the period. Rhudde was also vehemently opposed to the match and threatened to disinherit Maria. Their lengthy and tortured courtship was conducted primarily via correspondence and brief meetings, some permitted by the family and others clandestine. The elder Golding Constable's death in May 1816 marked a watershed, as his property was divided between his six children and Abram took control of the family business on the condition that he provide financial support for his five siblings. Constable expected to receive around £400 per year, which was adequate to support a family (though considered insufficient by Maria). On 2 July, the day of John and Mary Fisher's wedding, he resolved that he too would marry, and on 2 October 1816, after much equivocation on both sides, John and Maria were married by John Fisher at St-Martin-in-the-Fields in London.

The Constables had an extended honeymoon, spending six weeks with John and Mary Fisher in Osmington, near Weymouth, where Fisher had a parish, and also visiting Bishop Fisher in Salisbury and Mary Fisher's father, a cleric himself, in Berkshire. Constable drew and painted the coastal landscape energetically, his works including a vivid oil sketch and painting of Weymouth Bay, which he may have worked on simultaneously (pp.52, 53). Back in London in 1817, Constable took a lease on 1 Keppel Street, Bloomsbury, and in the summer he and Maria spent three months in East Bergholt where Constable worked outside intensively, knowing that

Maria Bicknell, Mrs John Constable 1816
Oil paint on canvas
30.5 × 25.1

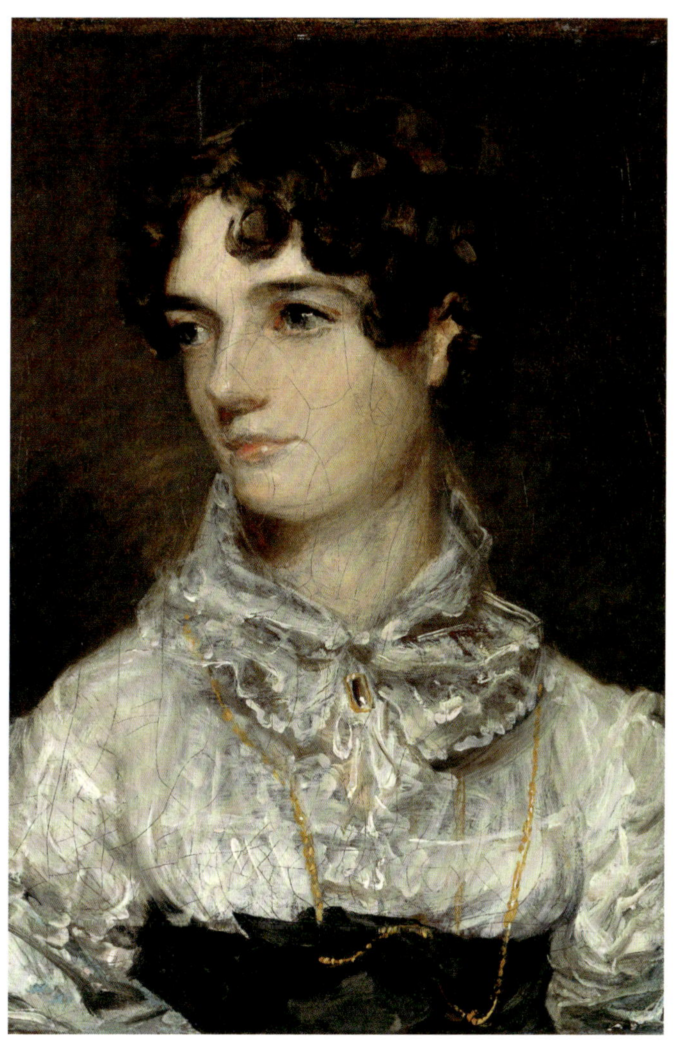

he would be unlikely to have another extended visit there since the family house was to be sold and his siblings dispersed. Maria had had a miscarriage earlier in the year, but in December gave birth to their first child, John Charles. Although she had tuberculosis, Maria would have a total of seven children in ten years, irreparably damaging her already delicate health, and straining the family's finances. London was notoriously polluted, and the Constables' efforts to find healthier locations close to the metropolis led them to rent

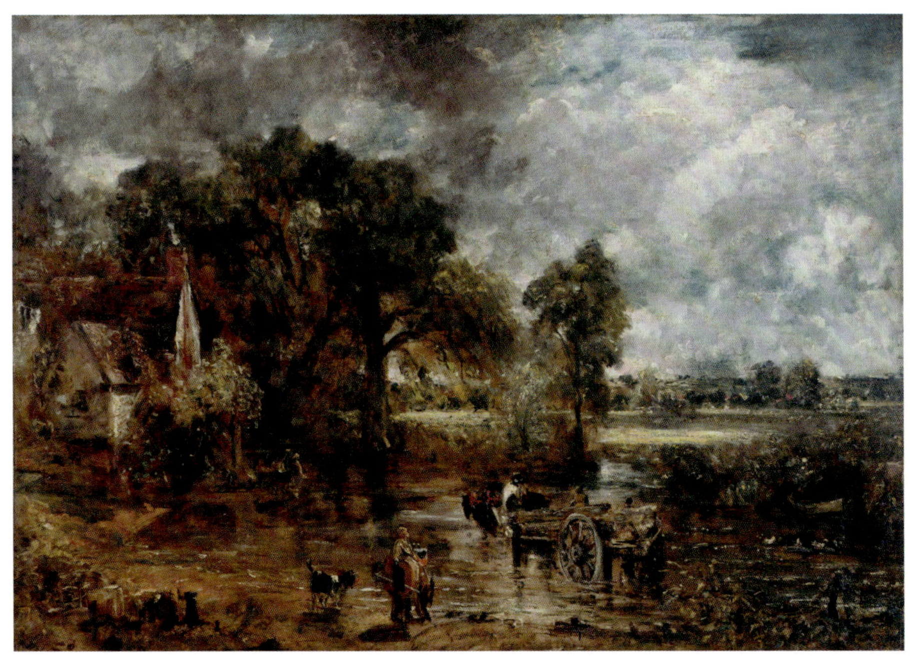

houses in Hampstead from the summer of 1819 onwards,
as well as in Brighton between 1824 and 1828, while still
maintaining a house and studio in London. Maria also
regularly stayed with relatives in Putney. The Keppel Street
house proved too small to accommodate the growing family
comfortably, and in 1822 the Constables moved across
Tottenham Court Road to the house formerly owned by
Joseph Farington in Charlotte Street, where there was
a spacious studio.

Constable was a loving and attentive father, but as his
family expanded and Maria's health declined, the children
were increasingly cared for by servants, including the tutor
Charles Boner, and often sent away to stay with relatives for
lengthy periods. Between around 1820 and 1827, Constable
was assisted by Johnny Dunthorne, the able son of his former
mentor John Dunthorne, whose various duties included
preparing Constable's paints and palette, priming canvases,
tracing outlines of compositions on the six-footer canvases,
making copies of Constable's paintings, and even finishing
some of the paintings that had been languishing in the studio
– the 'dead horses', as Constable called them.

ABOVE
*Full-scale Study for
"The Hay Wain"* c.1821
Oil paint on canvas
137 × 188

OPPOSITE
The Hay Wain 1820–1,
exh.1821
Oil paint on canvas
130.2 × 185.4

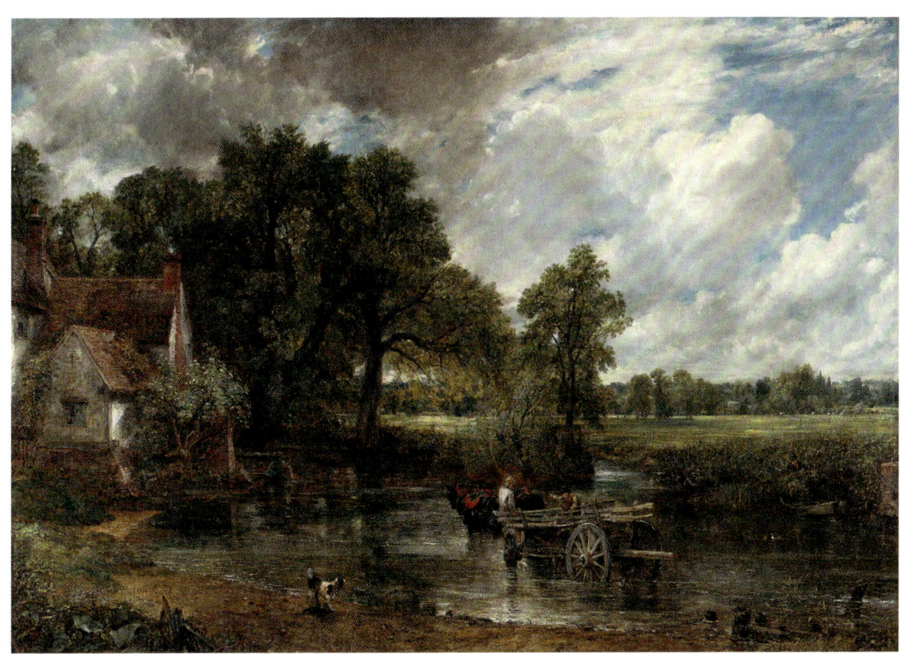

Although Constable found his peripatetic lifestyle and domestic responsibilities challenging in his post-marriage years, he was extremely productive, despite having to negotiate a fundamental transition from working en plein air to painting in the studio. In late 1818, he began work on a large canvas, the first of the 'six-footers' for which he is now famous, using earlier sketches and paintings as raw material.[13] This was *A Scene on the River Stour* exh.1819, now known as *The White Horse* (p.62). Constable sent paintings to the major annual exhibitions at the Royal Academy and British Institution, and had recognised the need to make larger and distinctively coloured works that would stand out on the densely hung walls. He was likely influenced by the large paintings that Turner and John Martin were exhibiting; in 1818, for example, Turner showed three paintings at the Royal Academy, two of which, *Dort or Dordrecht, the Dort Packet-Boat from Rotterdam becalmed* 1818 and *The Field of Waterloo* 1818, measured over seven feet wide apiece.

Constable's first six-footer was well received, and he was elected as an Associate of the Royal Academy on 1 November. (The family finances were also bolstered that year as Maria's grandfather, the infamous Dr Rhudde, died in May, bequeathing her and her children £4,000.) Thereafter, Constable set out to produce and exhibit one large painting each year, an objective he fulfilled until 1832, with the exception of 1823, when he experienced many 'interruptions' and exhibited a smaller painting, *Salisbury Cathedral from the Bishop's Grounds*, which John Fisher senior had commissioned (p.70). The first six – *The White Horse* as well as *Stratford Mill* 1819–20 (p.63), *The Hay Wain* (pp.2, 22), *View on the Stour, near Dedham* c.1822–6, *A Boat Passing a Lock* 1826 (p.78), and *The Leaping Horse* 1825 (p.73) depicted the river Stour. Three more were Suffolk scenes: *The Cornfield* exh.1826 (p.32), *Dedham Vale* ?1827–8 (p.79) and *Helmington Dell* 1825–6. The others – *Chain Pier, Brighton* exh.1827 (pp.76–7), *Hadleigh Castle* exh.1829 (p.83), *Salisbury Cathedral from the Meadows* exh.1831 (pp.80–1) and *The Opening of Waterloo Bridge* exh.1832 (pp.84–5) – depicted locations with which Constable had developed a deep personal connection, associating them with different periods in his life. Taken together, they form a kind of autobiography.

Constable struggled with working on a large scale in the studio and, for all but three of these paintings, he used existing drawings and paintings to make a study of identical size on a piece of canvas that he pinned up for reference when painting the exhibited work.[14] This method of working, which he had first employed for *The White Horse*, seems to have been unique to him, and was labour-intensive and costly in terms of canvas and materials. Twentieth-century critics often preferred these expressive full-size studies to the finished paintings, but Constable never exhibited or tried to sell them. He usually also exhibited several smaller paintings.

The art world of the period was a notoriously hostile environment, in which artists competed for patronage and some critics vied with each other to write lacerating reviews. No artist went unscathed; Turner, for example, was regularly subjected to brutal critique, though he brushed it off dismissively by saying that all criticism was 'useless'. Although his large paintings received mostly positive reviews, Constable was routinely excoriated for their coarseness and lack of finish, and, from 1821 onwards, for 'spottiness', which referred to the scumbling, or marks he made by dragging dry white paint across the canvas to create highlights. Constable reacted angrily to negative comments. His own view on the appearance of his paintings was complex, however; although

roughness was a crucial feature of his practice, he himself
did not regard his paintings as finished at the time they
were exhibited. He typically painted feverishly up until the
deadline for submission, and brought the paintings back
to the studio after the exhibition to work further on them.

Sales for the six-footers were patchy, and the majority
languished in Constable's studio after being exhibited.
Nor were they profitable: John Fisher bought *The White Horse*
in 1819 for 100 guineas, and *The Lock* sold immediately at the
1824 exhibition for 150 guineas, but these prices were low
in comparison with those charged by Turner, who by
1811 was typically selling large paintings for 400 guineas.
Interest in large-scale paintings of everyday rural scenes
was very limited; British collectors preferred either
landscapes or genre paintings on a small scale or, on
sizeable canvases, portraits or grander historical subjects.
The art market was also severely impacted by the financial
crash of 1825–6, which had global repercussions.

FRENCH CONNECTIONS

Admiration for Constable's unconventional approach to
painting was to come from across the Channel, however.
In 1821 the painter Théodore Géricault and critic Charles
Nodier, visiting London from Paris, saw *The Hay Wain* at
the Royal Academy, Géricault later telling Eugène Delacroix
that he was 'stunned' by Constable's unorthodox brushwork
and colour. Nodier's positive critical assessments of
Constable's work generated interest in France, and in 1824
the French dealer John Arrowsmith bought *The Hay Wain*,
along with *View on the Stour, near Dedham* and a smaller
painting of Yarmouth, for £250, and another French dealer,
Claude Schroth, commissioned paintings to sell in Paris.

Arrowsmith also arranged for the two six-footers and
a small painting of Hampstead to be shown at the *Salon*,
the annual exhibition of work of living artists at the
Louvre, in the summer of 1824. They created a sensation,
and Constable was awarded a Gold Medal, the highest
honour. Constable's French connections were short-
lived, however; in November 1825 he abruptly terminated
his relationship with Arrowsmith due to the dealer's
alleged 'impertinence', and in the following year financial
difficulties prevented Schroth from commissioning any
more works.

HAMPSTEAD

Despite spending lengthy periods in the studio, Constable still found time to sketch outdoors on visits to East Bergholt and Salisbury, and from 1819, in Hampstead, where the Constables rented a house each summer and, from 1827, all year round. Hampstead was then on the periphery of London, and living there enabled Constable to 'unite a town & country life'.[15] In 1821 and 1822, Constable painted a large number of studies of clouds outdoors, using oil paints on paper, a practice he described as 'skying' (pp.64–5).[16] He meticulously dated these sketches, often adding observations about the weather conditions, which revealed his sustained passion for close observation of nature and interest in the developing science of meteorology. 'Skying' also had an emotional resonance for Constable, who described the sky as 'the chief organ of sentiment'.

He also painted several views of Hampstead Heath (pp.68–9, 86, 90–1), though does not seem to have considered it an appropriate subject for a six-footer. He continued to make small oil sketches outdoors, having devised a method of preparation: gluing two sheets of thick paper together and priming them before venturing out to paint. These small but powerful works are remarkable for their expressive spontaneity.

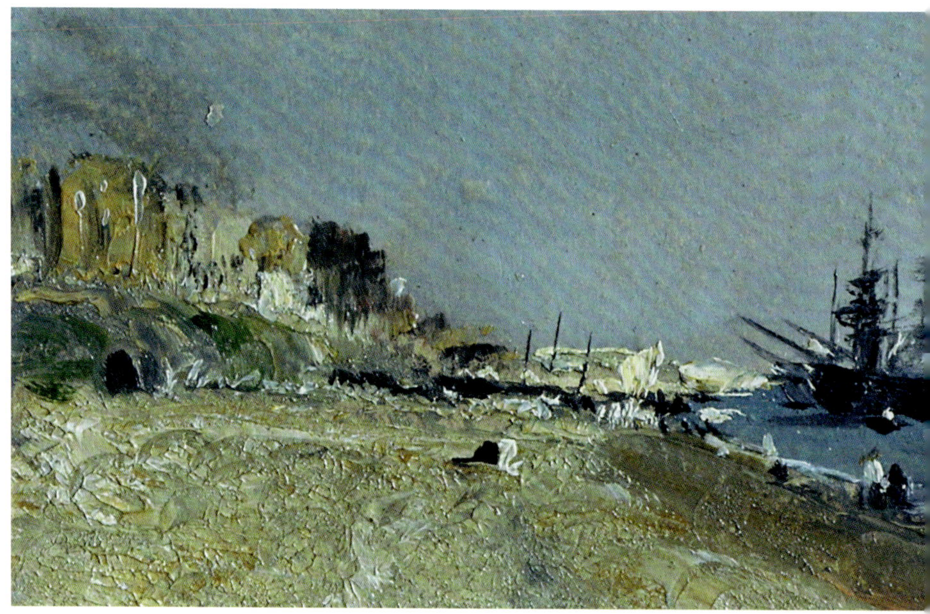

Brighton Beach with Colliers
1824
Oil on paper
14.6 × 24.8

Maria's health continued to deteriorate, and in May 1824 Constable moved her with their four children and two servants to Brighton in the hope that fresh air and sea bathing would be restorative. Brighton was just fifty miles from London, and there was a good coach service between the cities that Constable used for regular visits.

Brighton was a busy, fashionable resort. Constable complained about its pretentiousness and noisiness, but he was fascinated by the working life of the shore and made numerous pencil drawings and vivid oil sketches of fishing boats and colliers (boats used to transport coal) (below). He also sketched the Royal Suspension Chain Pier, a modern iron structure that had been recently constructed to serve as a landing-stage for packet boats from Dieppe. In 1827, Constable exhibited a large painting of the Chain Pier at the Royal Academy, a modern subject that was a significant departure from his timeless rural scenes (pp.76–7). The work was unenthusiastically received and remained in Constable's studio until his death. Turner, however, seems to have taken note, as shortly afterwards he painted in response *Brighton from the Sea* c.1829 for his patron Lord Egremont, a shareholder in the pier.

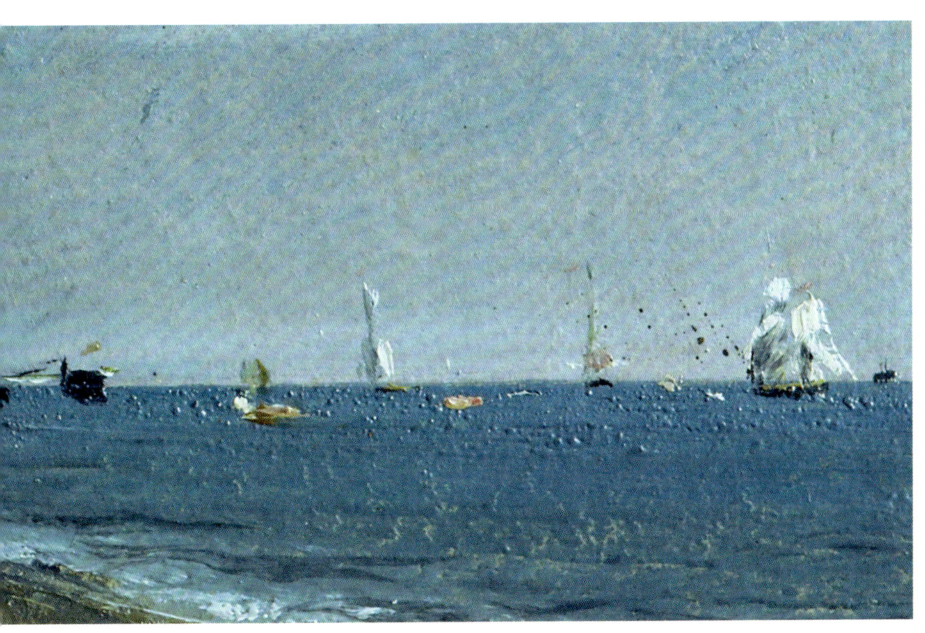

Maria gave birth to the couple's last child, Lionel, on 2 January 1828 in Hampstead, and died the following November at the age of forty-one. By an unkind stroke of fate, her death came only months after the death of her father brought a bequest of £20,000, ensuring that the family's financial troubles were over.

Constable was devastated by Maria's death, but channelled his grief into painting, embarking on a six-footer for which he had made a full-size study. He exhibited the painting at the Royal Academy the following May with the title *Hadleigh Castle, The Mouth of the Thames – Morning after a Stormy Night* (p.83). The subject was a ruined thirteenth-century castle in Essex, fifty miles from East Bergholt, overlooking the Nore, a submerged sandbank where the Thames meets the North Sea. Constable had visited Hadleigh in 1814, at a low point in his courtship of Maria, and the site had melancholy associations for him. The coloration is muted and the windswept landscape desolate, though the rays of sun penetrating the grey clouds following the storm seem to strike a more optimistic note. Constable had been elected a Royal Academician in February with a majority of a single vote, a result greeted unenthusiastically by most of his peers, and was apprehensive about the reception of the painting, but the critics were generally appreciative, commending its 'power, truth, and freshness', though most commented on the spottiness of the surface, which Turner had mischievously compared to whitewash.[17]

Shortly after Maria's death, Constable embarked on a series of mezzotint prints entitled *Various Subjects of Landscape, Characteristic of English Scenery, from Pictures Painted by John Constable, R.A.* (known as *English Landscape Scenery*). The undertaking was inspired by Turner's *Liber Studiorum*, a publication of landscape prints made with etching and mezzotint that the artist self-published between 1807 and 1819 (opposite).[18] Constable hoped that his project would generate public and critical recognition, and worked obsessively on the proofs. With mezzotint, the surface of the plate is textured or 'rocked' by passing a tool called a rocker over it in close, regular, lines, producing tiny points of metal known as 'burr'. When rocked all over, the plate will print as an area of continuous darkness. The engraver removes burr to create light areas using burnishers, scrapers

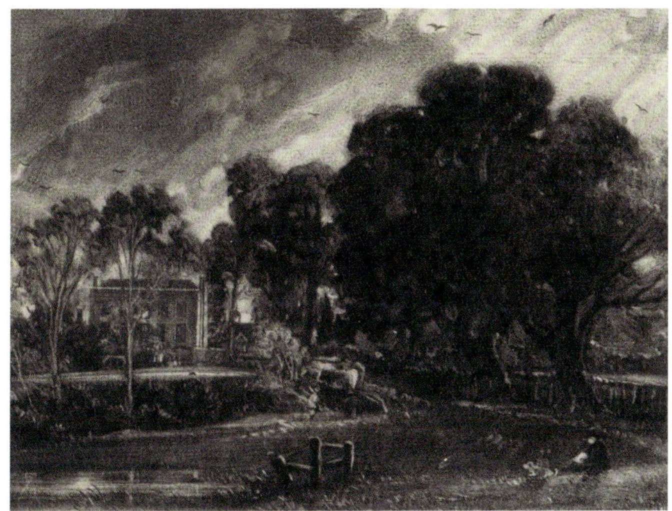

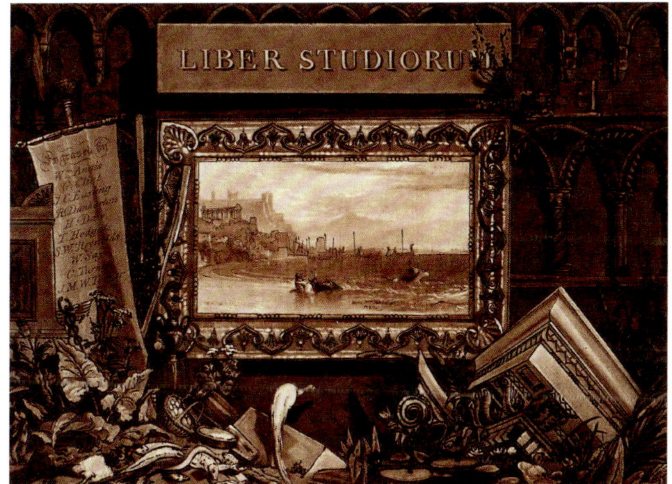

and polishers. Constable's choice of mezzotint to translate his images was appropriate since he was preoccupied with the rendering of chiaroscuro, or light and shade, which he came to see not only as a means of articulating space but as a principle of nature itself. In 1833, he added a new subtitle to *English Landscape Scenery: Principally Intended to Mark the Phenomena of the Chiaroscuro of Nature.* All the sites depicted had personal significance for Constable, and the series, like the sequence of six-footers, functions as a visual autobiography.

The frontispiece, *East Bergholt, Suffolk*, depicts Constable's birthplace and includes the seated figure of the sketching artist. The Latin epigraph from an unidentified source was translated by John Fisher:

> *This spot saw the day spring of my Life*
> *Hours of Joy, and years of Happiness,*
> *This place first tinged my boyish fancy with a love of art,*
> *This place was the origin of my Fame.*

Constable hired the twenty-seven-year-old David Lucas to engrave the prints, and the two worked in close (and often fraught) collaboration. Unlike Turner, who usually produced watercolours specifically for engravings, Constable provided Lucas with existing works in various media and scales, ranging from sketches to exhibited six-footers. These models functioned only as starting points, however, and as the numerous progress proofs reveal, the images evolved during the engraving process, under Constable's close supervision. Although the series received some positive reviews when it was launched in 1830, the critics disliked the coarseness of these richly textured prints, which are today acclaimed for their expressiveness.

THE 'CHURCH UNDER A CLOUD'

As Constable worked with Lucas on the prints, he was also consumed by anxieties regarding the state of the nation and the Anglican Church. At a time when liberalism was gaining momentum, Constable's politics were extremely conservative; paradoxically, they grew more reactionary as his work became increasingly avant-garde.

The 1820s and 1830s were decades of social and political turmoil. Britain was the most industrialised nation in the world, and agriculture itself had become more mechanised, with concentrated land ownership, large farms and scientific forms of land management and stock breeding that depressed rural employment and wages. In 1832, resistance to mechanisation among agricultural workers in the south of England culminated in the Captain Swing riots. Even though Constable claimed to never read a newspaper, he received anxious bulletins from Abram regarding local unrest in Suffolk, and seems to have been well aware of the bigger national picture. Regardless, he continued to produce tranquil rural scenes depicting

traditional agricultural practices – highly constructed images
that contradict his claims to be a 'natural painter' producing
a true and unmediated representation of rural life, as scholars
working in the late twentieth century demonstrated.[19]

Popular agitation for electoral reform, seeking to increase
the number of men allowed to vote and to reflect the new
concentration of the population in under-represented
industrial cities, had also gained momentum, and in 1832, the
Reform Act was passed in response to sustained campaigning.
It had faced strong opposition from conservatives, and caused
Constable great anxiety, even though it only increased to
eighteen per cent of the total adult male population the
number who could vote in England and Wales. The majority
of the working classes, and all women, were still excluded from
the political process.

At the same time, Constable, Fisher and other conservative
Anglicans were troubled by pressure to curtail the clergy's
privileges, and viewed with dismay the passage of the 1829
Catholic Relief Act which enabled Catholics to work in
government and the civil service.

In July 1829, Constable visited Fisher in Salisbury and
made a series of drawings, evidently with the idea of making
a major painting. After his return, Fisher wrote to him,
expressing his opinion that 'the "Church under a cloud"
is the best subject you can take'.[20] Fisher set up an easel,
and it is likely that Constable worked on the full-size
sketch during a visit that November. He then laboured on
the painting for eighteen months, exhibiting it at the Royal
Academy in 1831 with the title *Salisbury Cathedral from the Meadows*
(pp.80–1).

The painting encapsulates Constable's major artistic
and personal preoccupations – the vigorous brushwork, close
observation of nature, idealised agricultural practices,
the flowing river (though the Avon rather than the Stour),
the Anglican Church in peril, and meteorology. The rainbow,
adding an element of hope amid the storm, was a late
addition, and although it appears naturalistic, could not
have materialised in the atmospheric conditions Constable
depicts.[21] Despite its mixed critical reception, Constable
considered *Salisbury Cathedral* his most important work.
In the meantime, the Reform Act received royal assent on
7 June, and Fisher died on 28 August at the age of thirty-four.

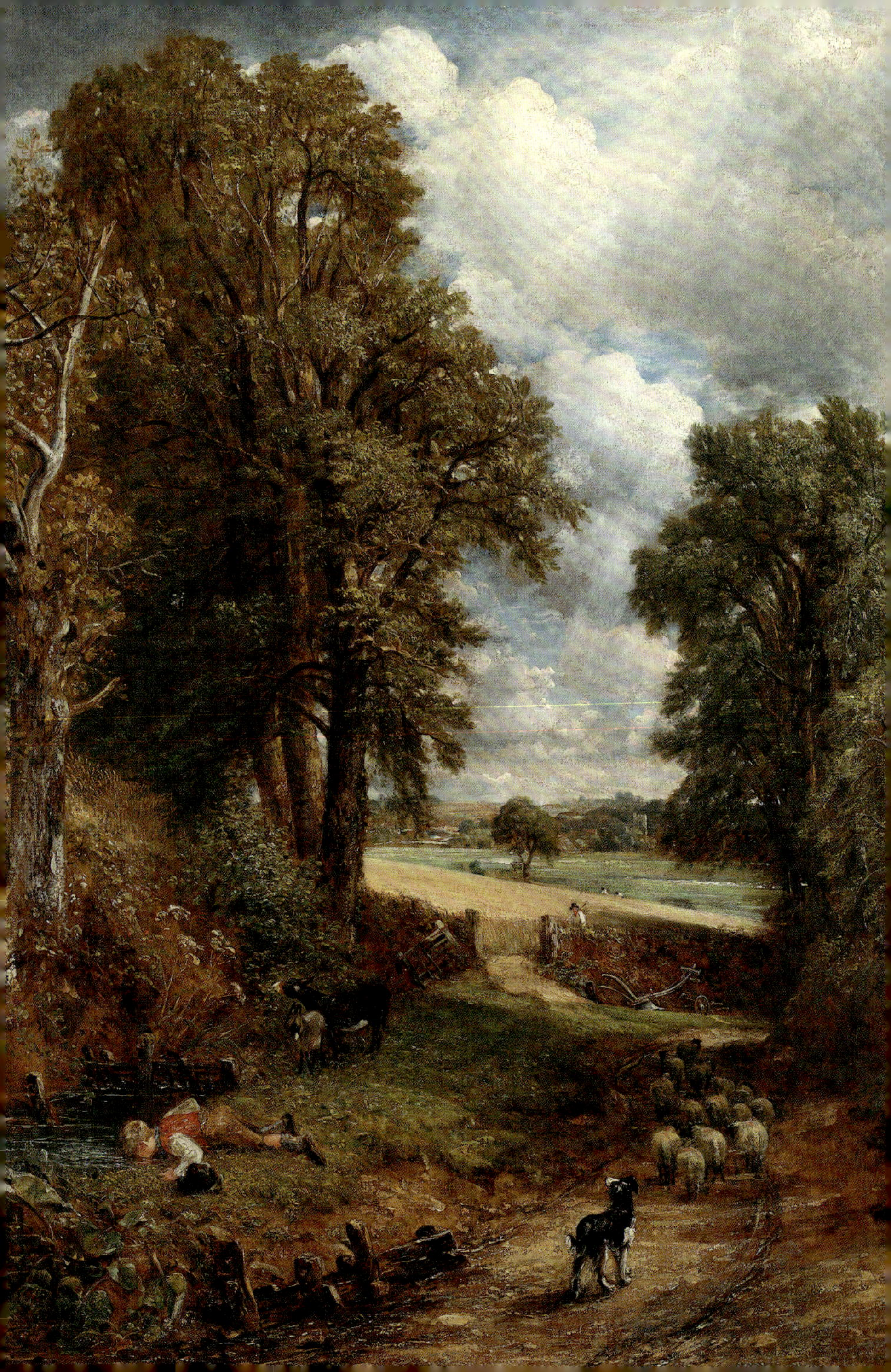

VALEDICTION

Constable died on 31 April 1837, having continued to exhibit at the Royal Academy every year until his death with the exception of 1834.[22] The last painting he exhibited at the Royal Academy, in 1836, *Cenotaph to the Memory of Sir Joshua Reynolds, erected in the grounds of Coleorton Hall, Leicestershire by the late Sir George Beaumont. Bt.*, was valedictory in tone (p.88). The monument to Reynolds is flanked by busts of Raphael and Michaelangelo, while the enigmatic figure of a stag looks back at the viewer.

1836 marked the final Royal Academy exhibition in Somerset House before a move to the National Gallery, and this sombre, elegiac painting was likely intended by Constable to mark the occasion. It also was an appropriate epitaph to Constable himself, though he could not have known that he would die the following year. After his death, a group of friends and admirers organised a subscription to buy *The Cornfield* (opposite) and present it to the National Gallery. This initiated a gradual process of appreciation of Constable's significance, which today is fully recognised.

The Cornfield
exh.1826
Oil paint on canvas
143 × 122

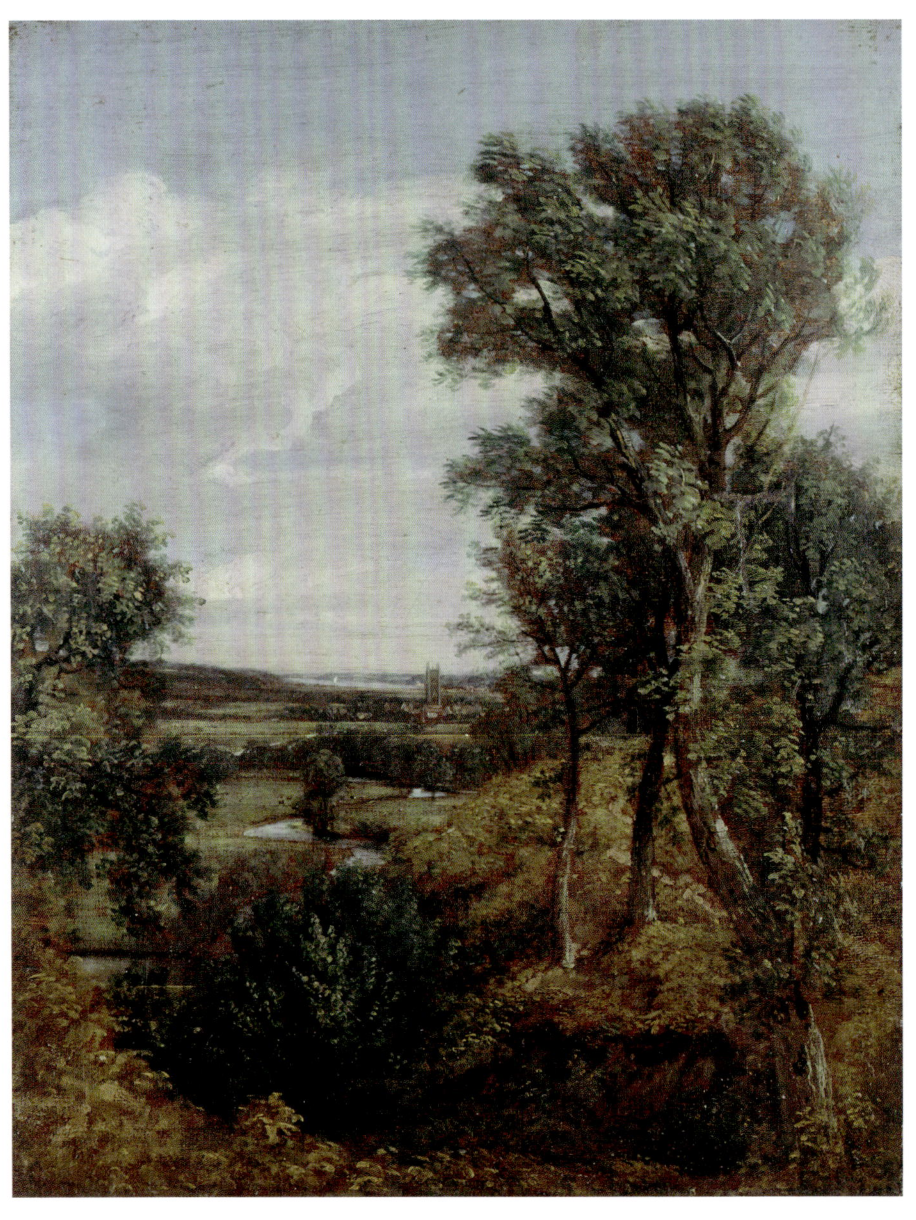

Dedham Vale 1802
Oil paint on canvas
43·5 × 34·4

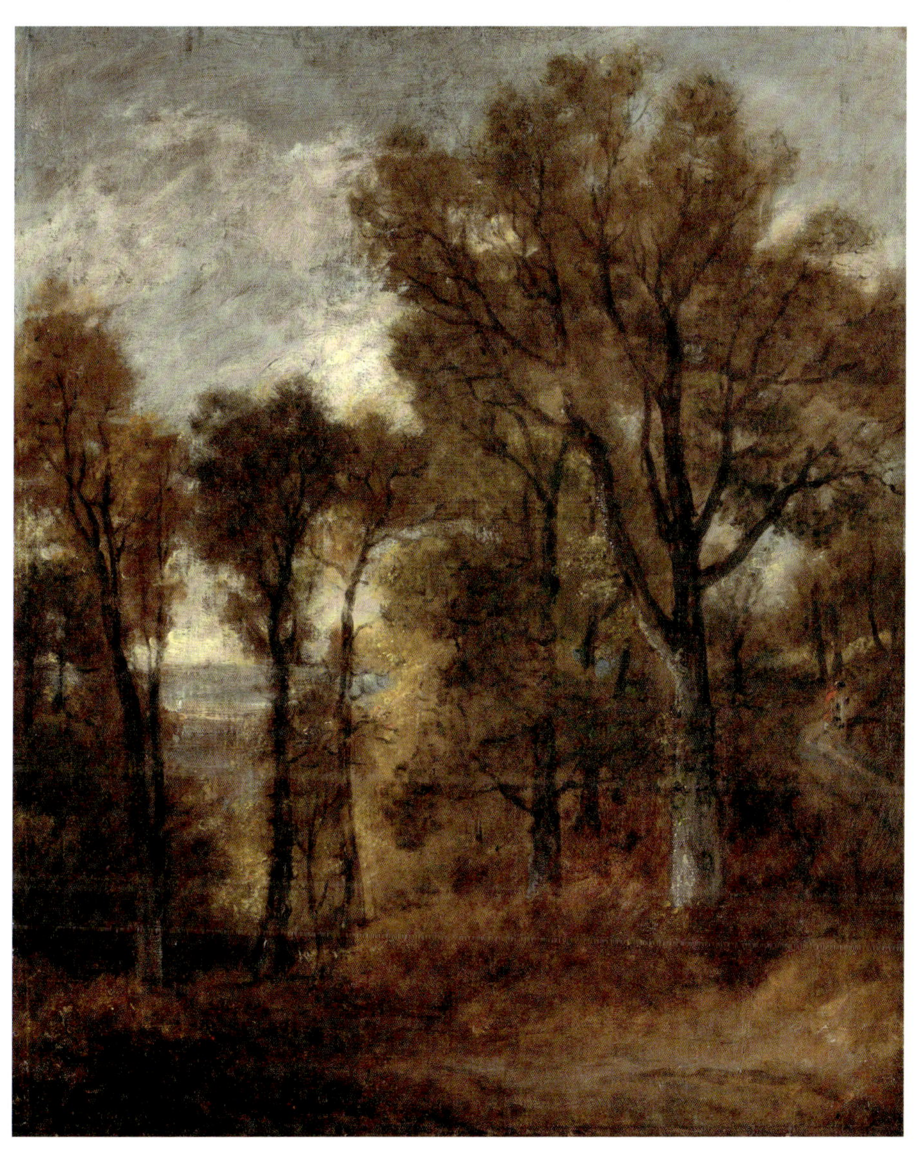

Woodland Scene overlooking
Dedham Vale c.1802–3
Oil paint on canvas
77 × 65

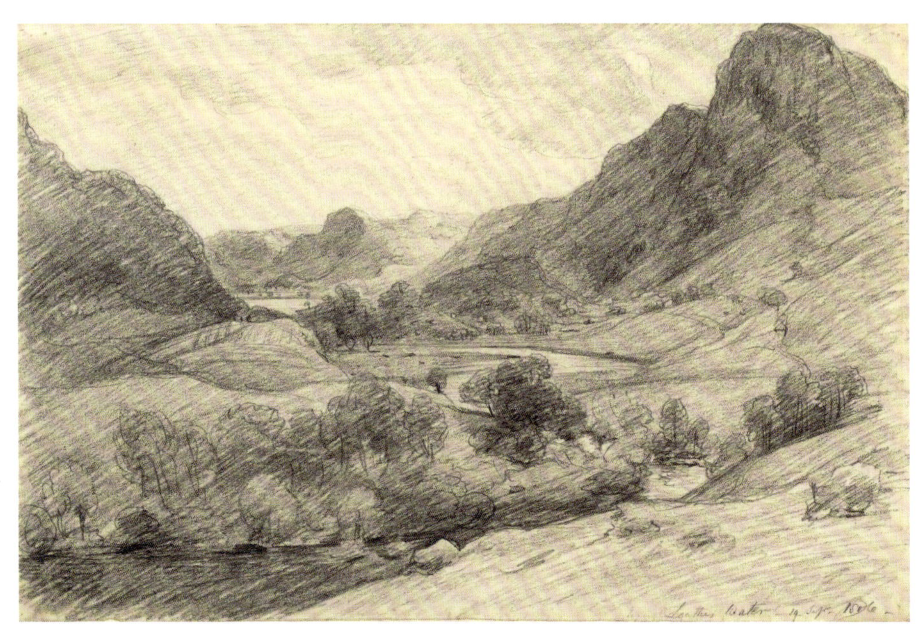

Leathes Water
(Thirlmere), 9 Sept. 1806
1806
Graphite on paper
25.1 × 38.8

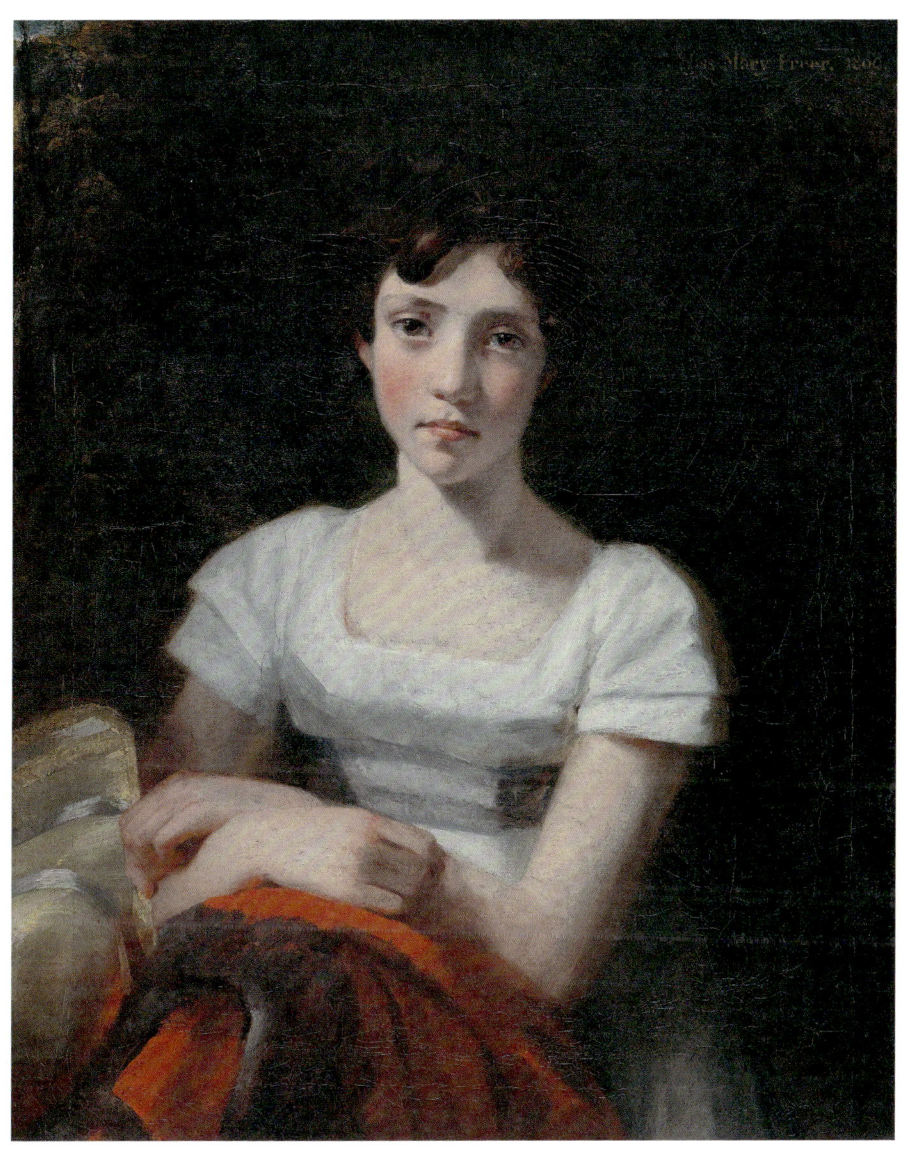

Mary Freer 1809
Oil paint on canvas
76.2 × 63.5

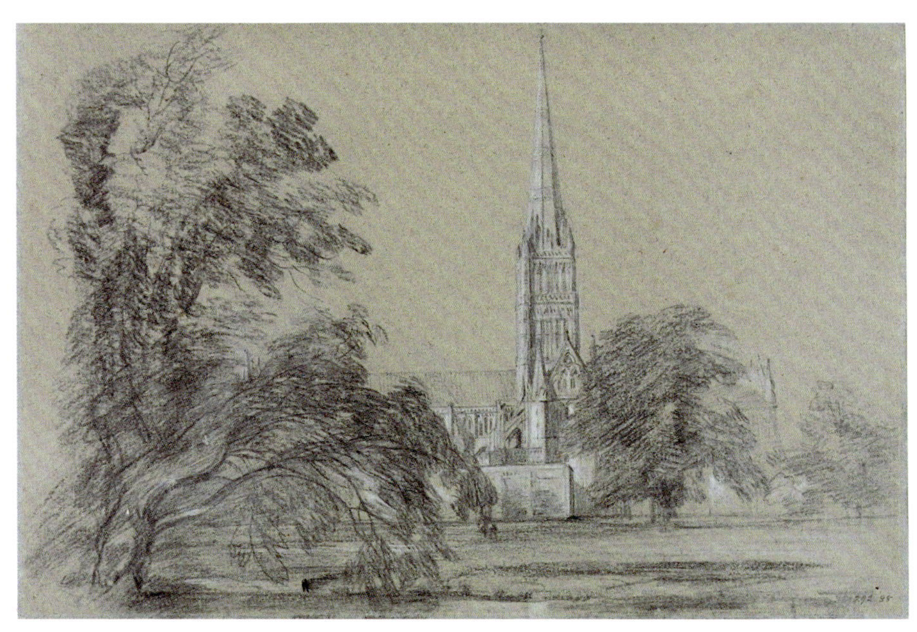

*Salisbury Cathedral from
the South-West* 1811
Chalk on paper
19.5 × 29.9

Summer Evening
1811–12, exh.1812
Oil paint on canvas
31.7 × 49.5

Peter Paul Rubens
The Rainbow Landscape c.1636
Oil paint on wood
137 × 235.5

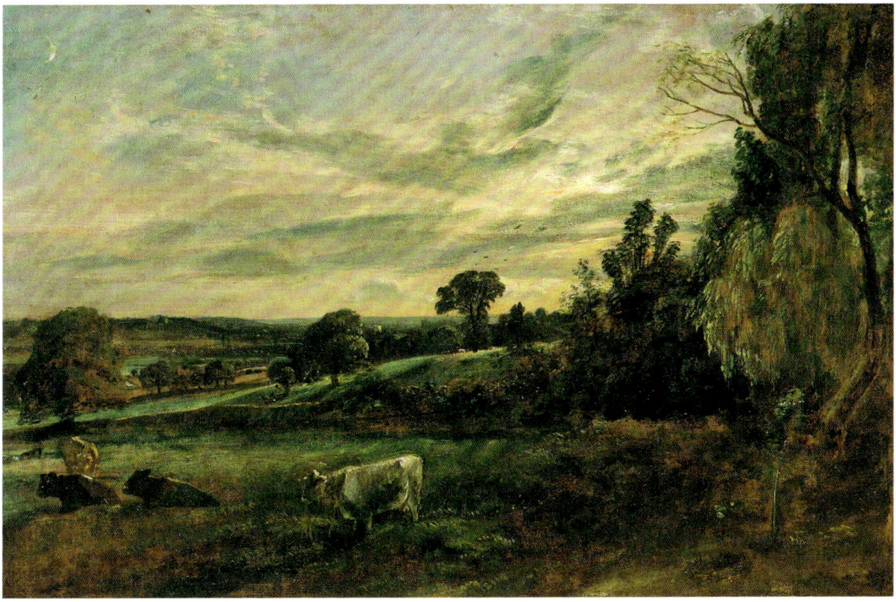

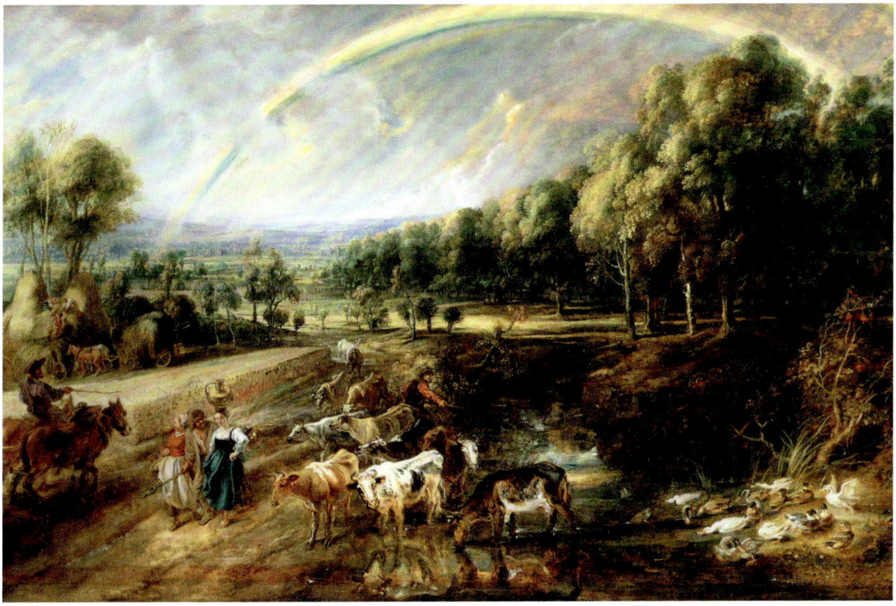

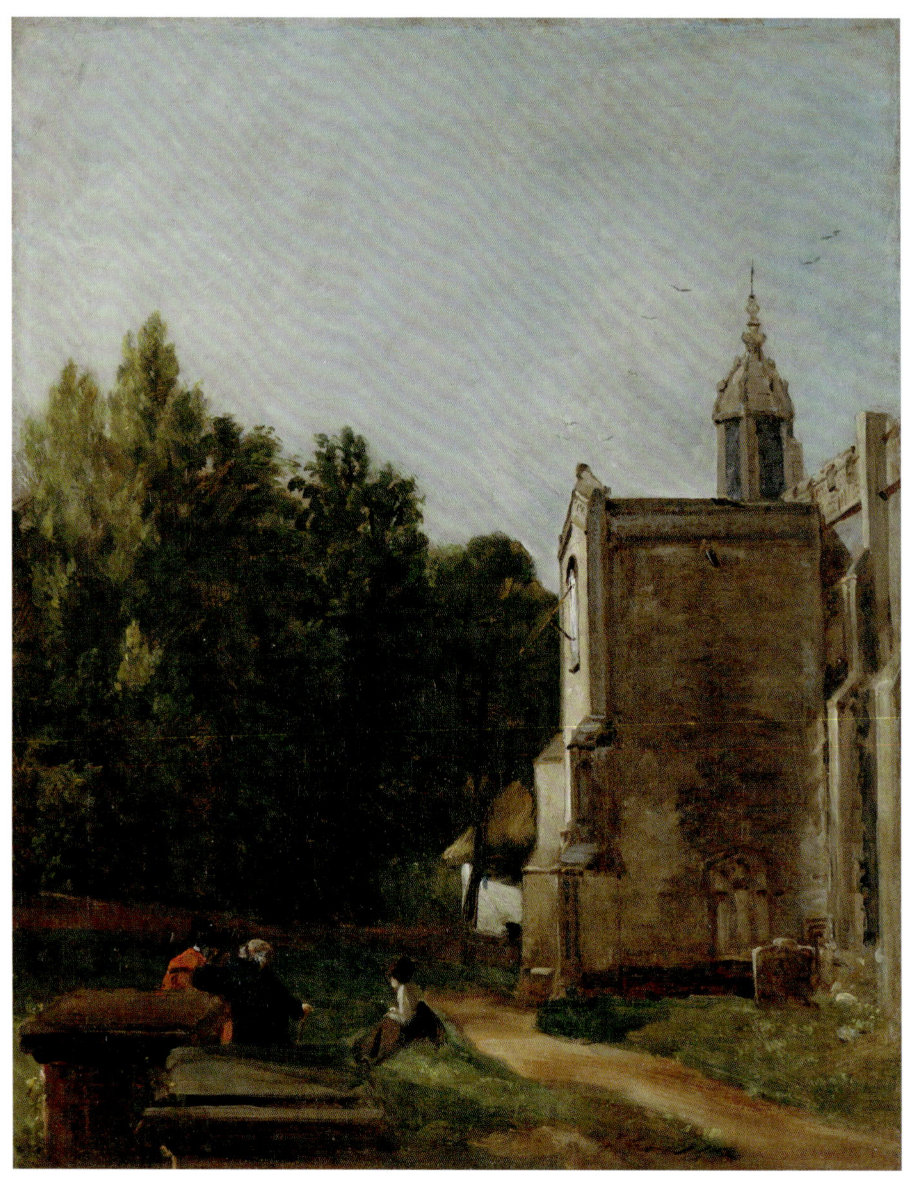

The Church Porch, East Bergholt
exh.1810
Oil paint on canvas
44.5 × 35.9

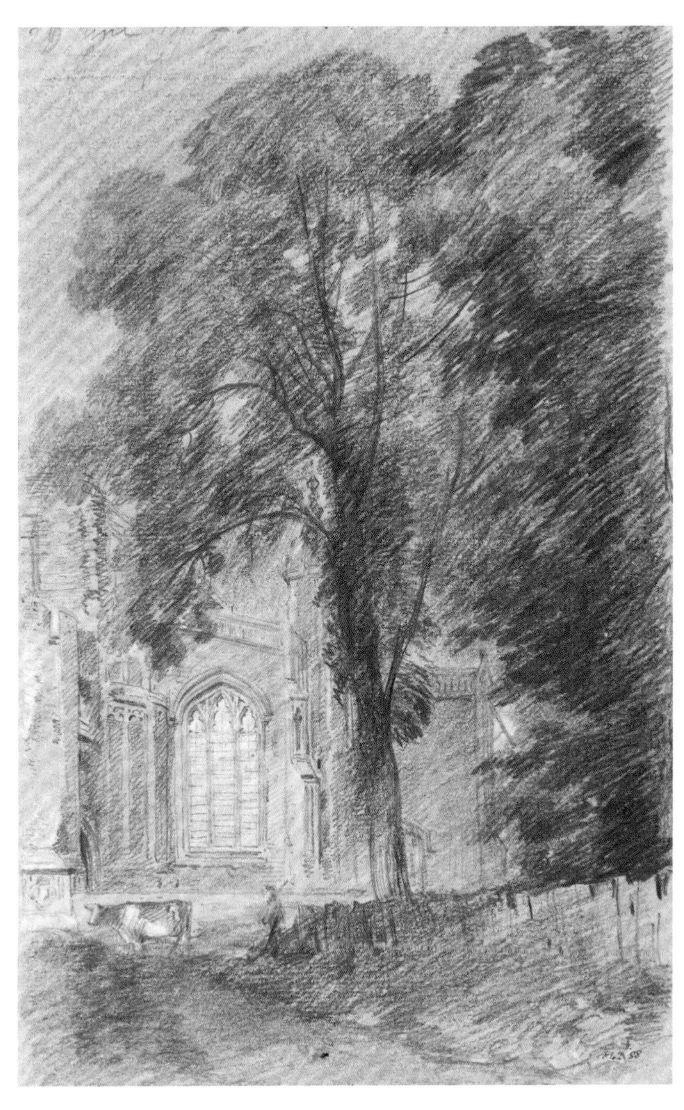

*East Bergholt Church, part
of the west end seen beyond
a group of elm trees* 1812
Chalk on paper
31 × 19.7

OVERLEAF
*The Stour Valley and Dedham
Village* 1814–15, exh.1815
Oil paint on canvas
55.6 × 77.8

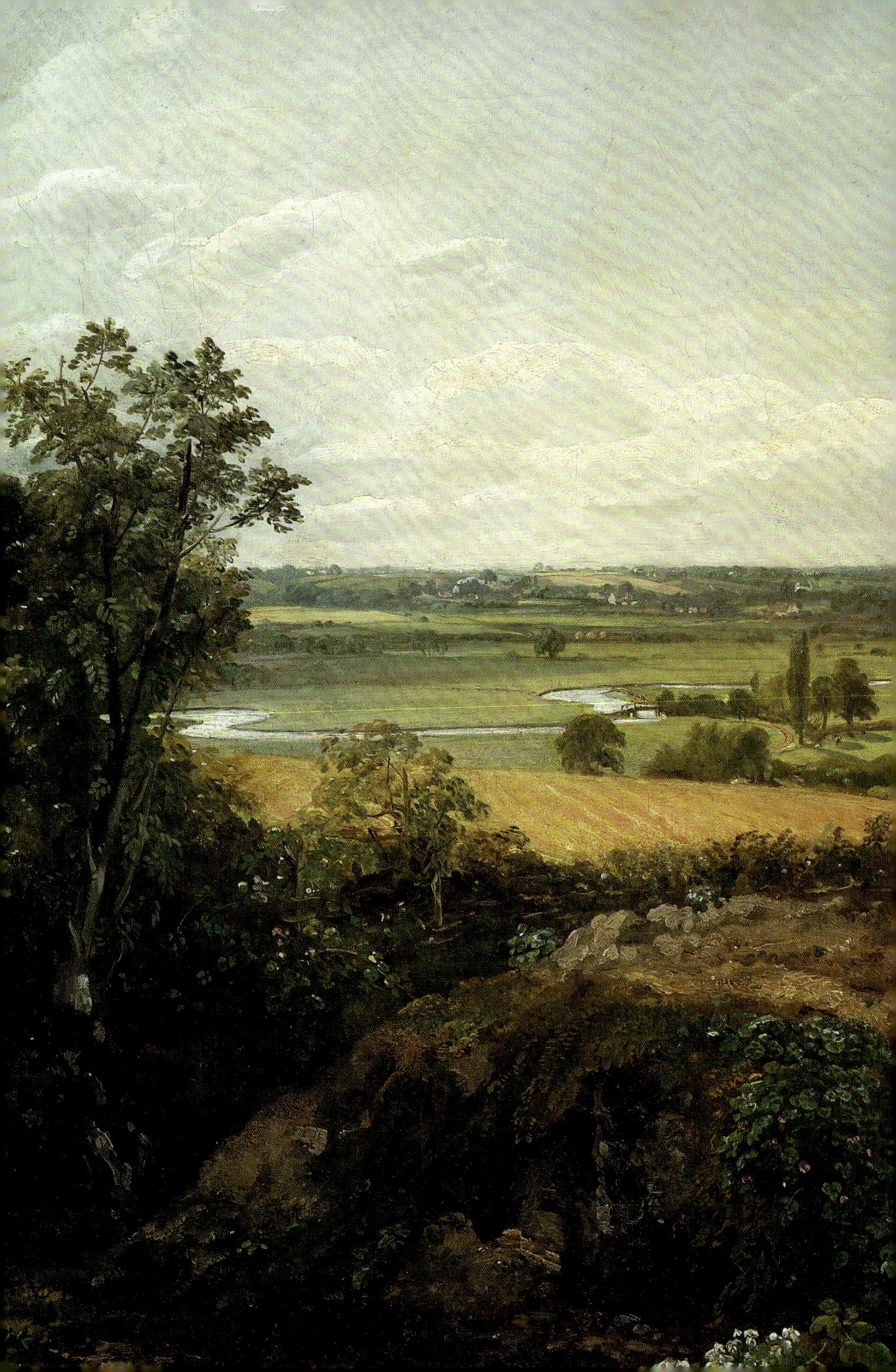

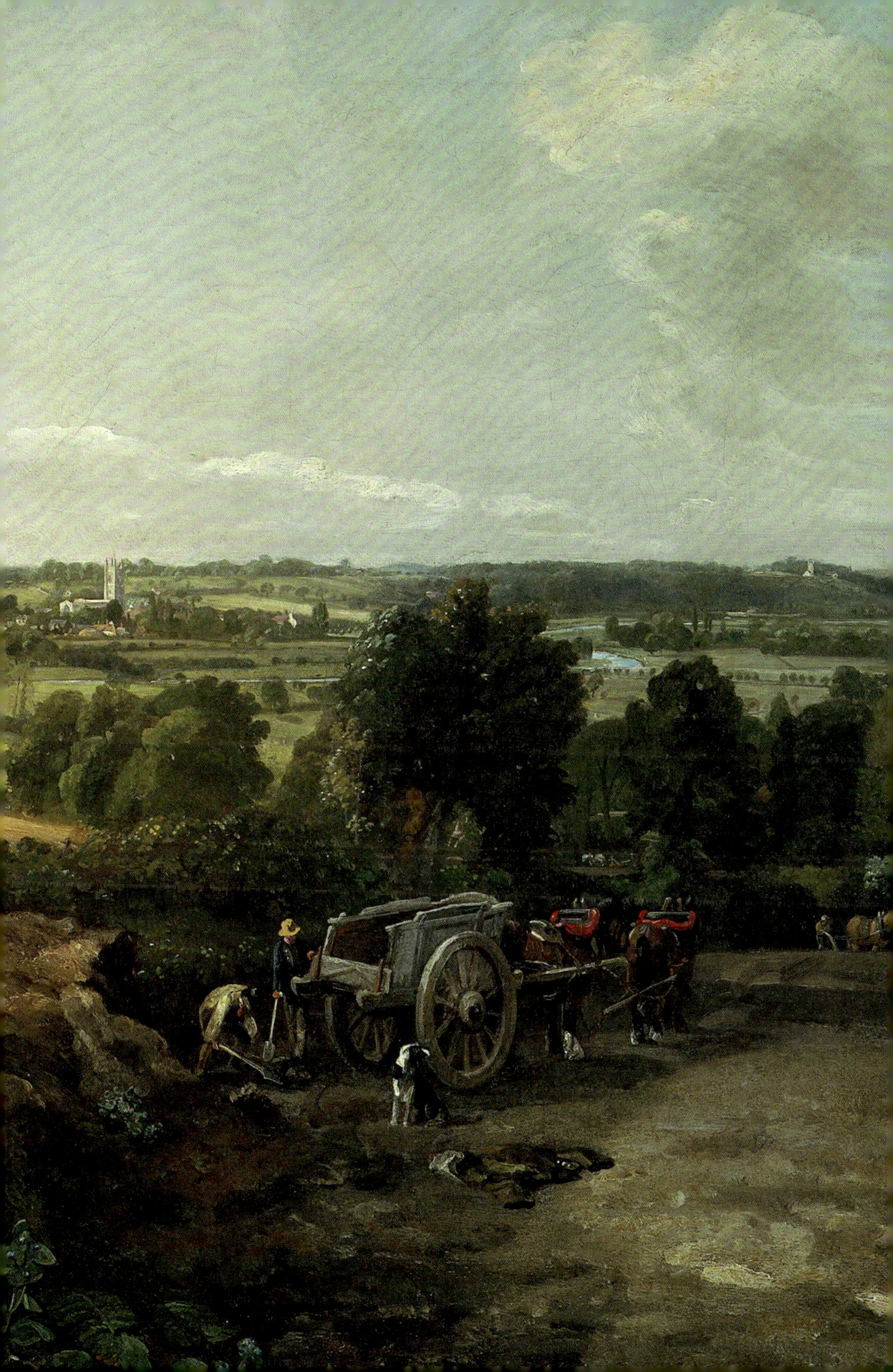

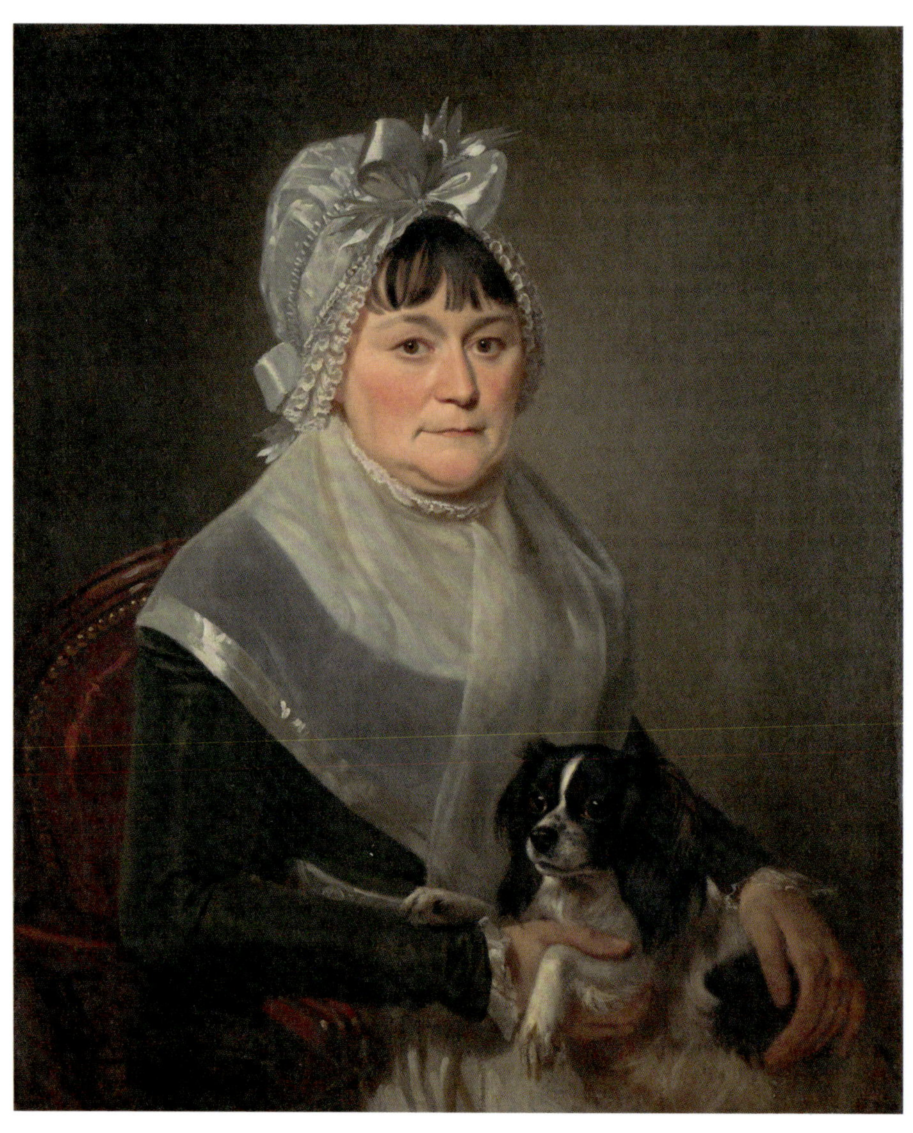

Ann Constable
1800–5 or 1815
Oil paint on canvas
76.5 × 63.9

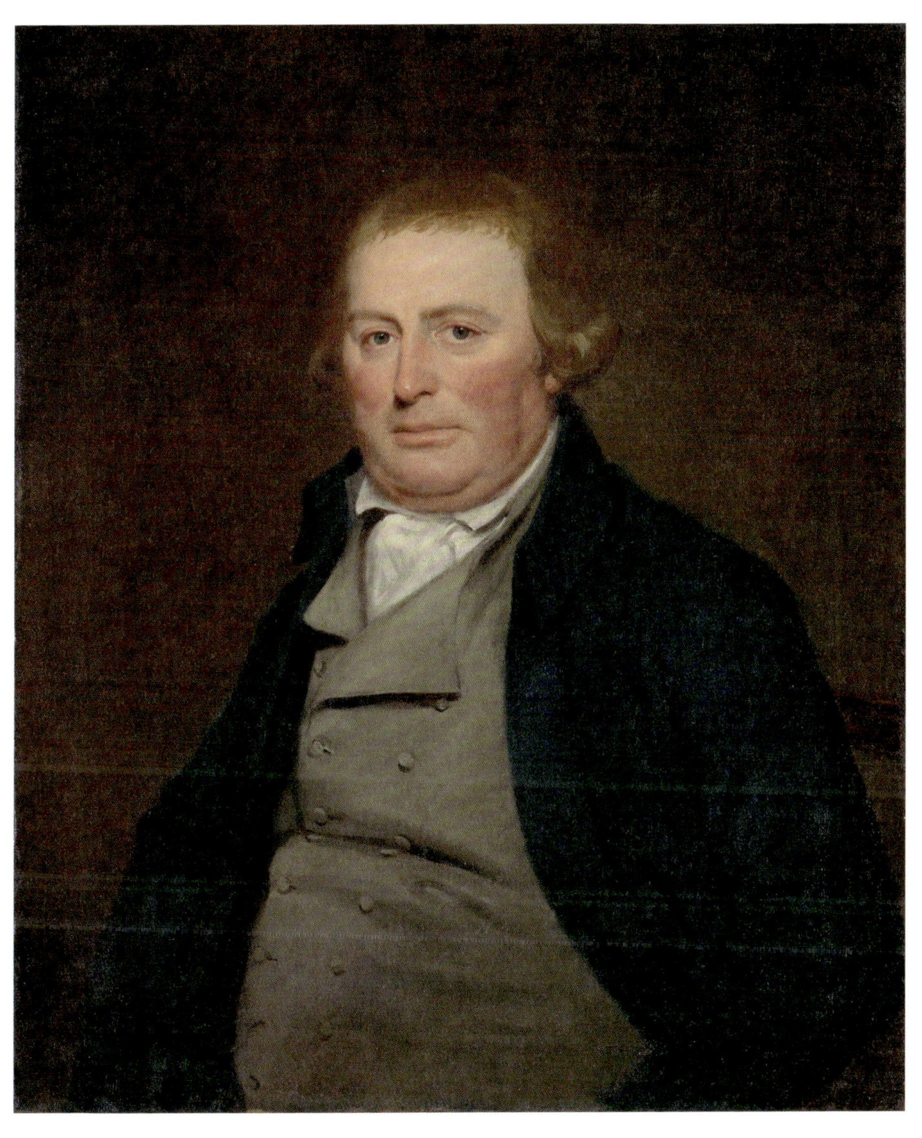

Golding Constable
1815
Oil paint on canvas
75.9 × 63.2

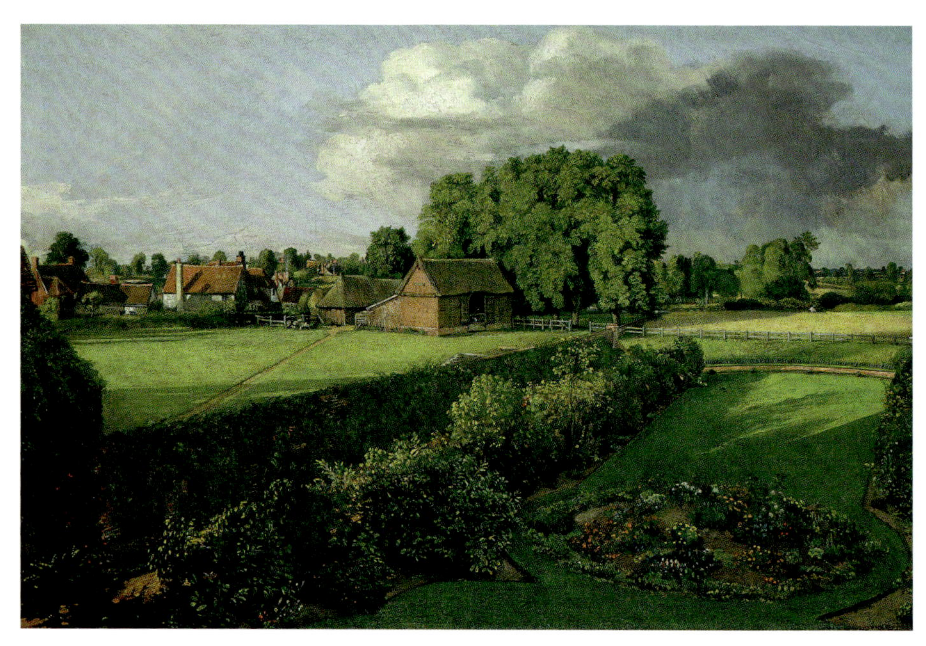

Golding Constable's Flower
Garden 1815
Oil paint on canvas
33 × 50.8

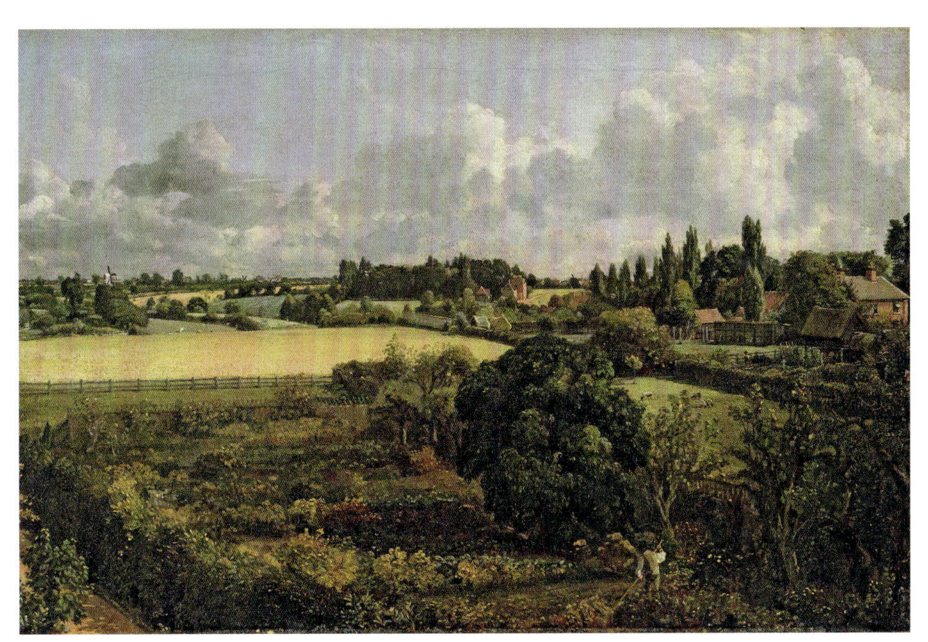

Golding Constable's Kitchen Garden 1815
Oil paint on canvas
33 × 50.8

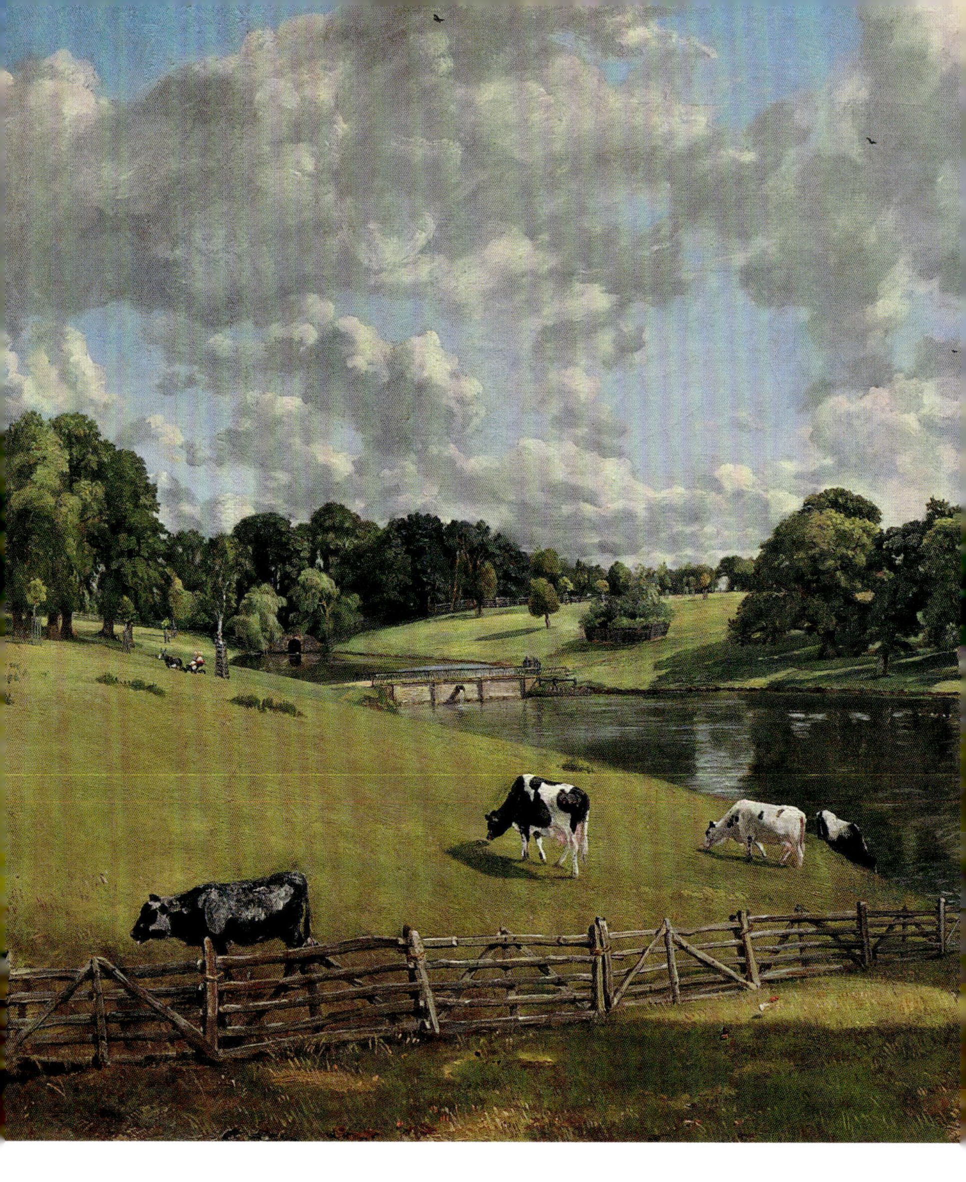

Wivenhoe Park 1816,
exh.1817
Oil paint on canvas
56.1 × 101.2

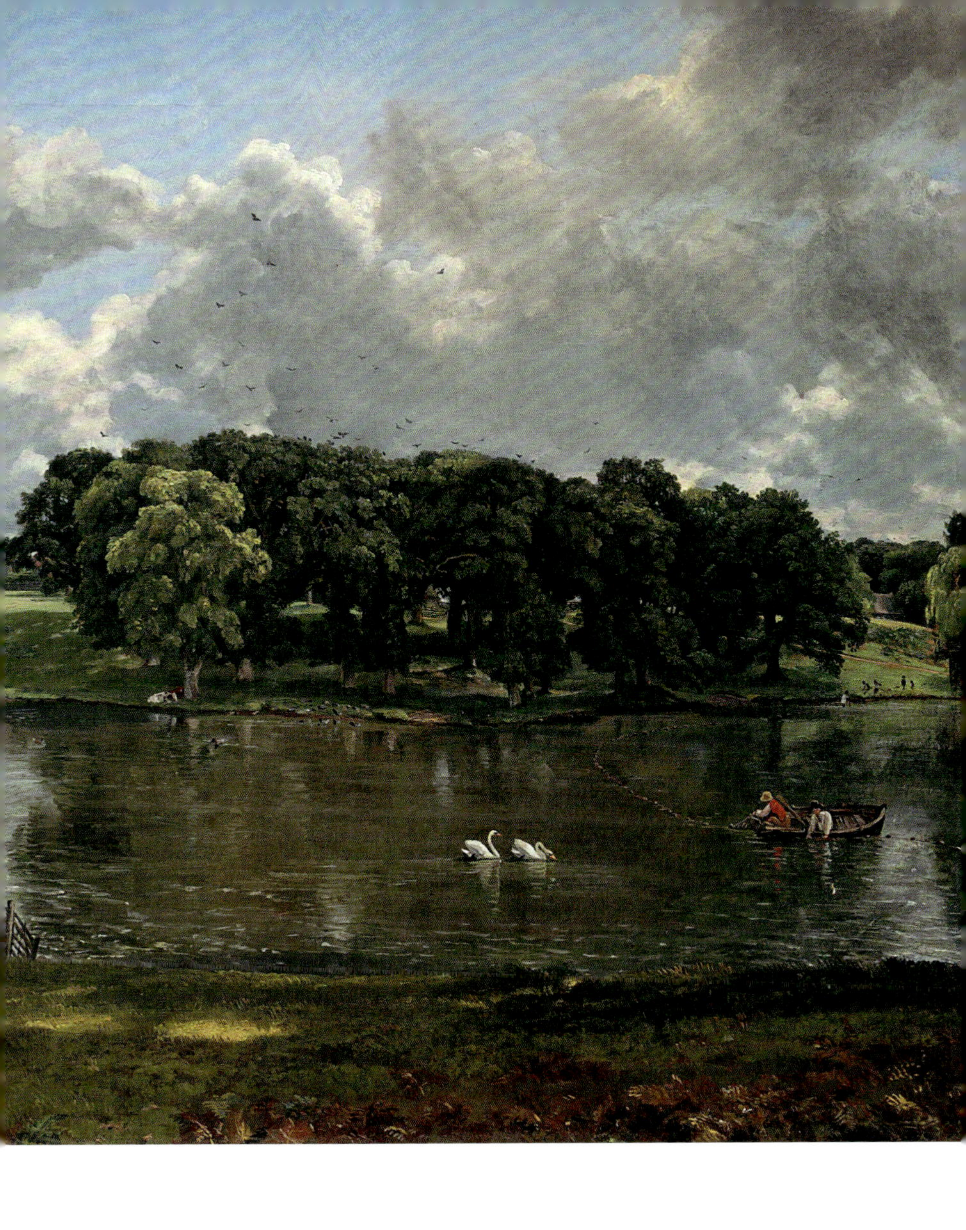

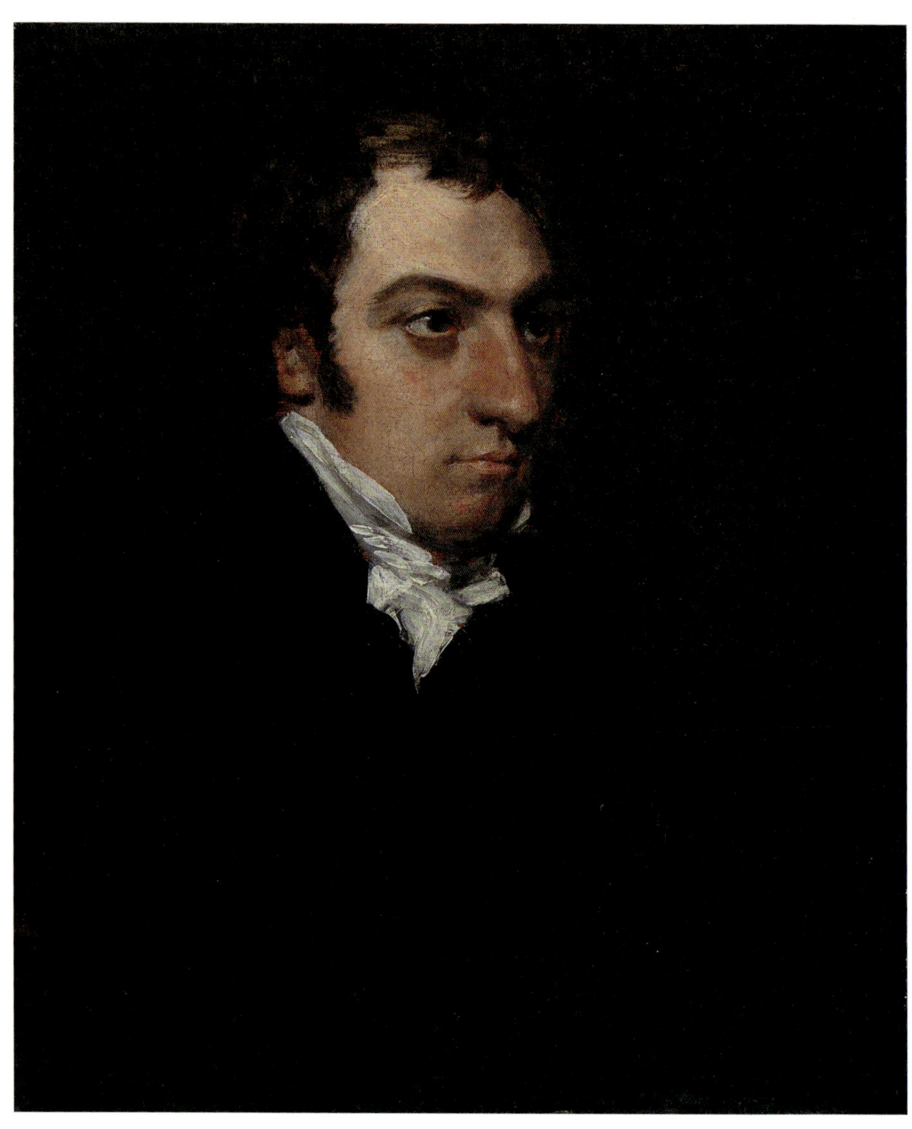

Archdeacon John Fisher
exh.1816
Oil paint on canvas
35.9 × 30.3

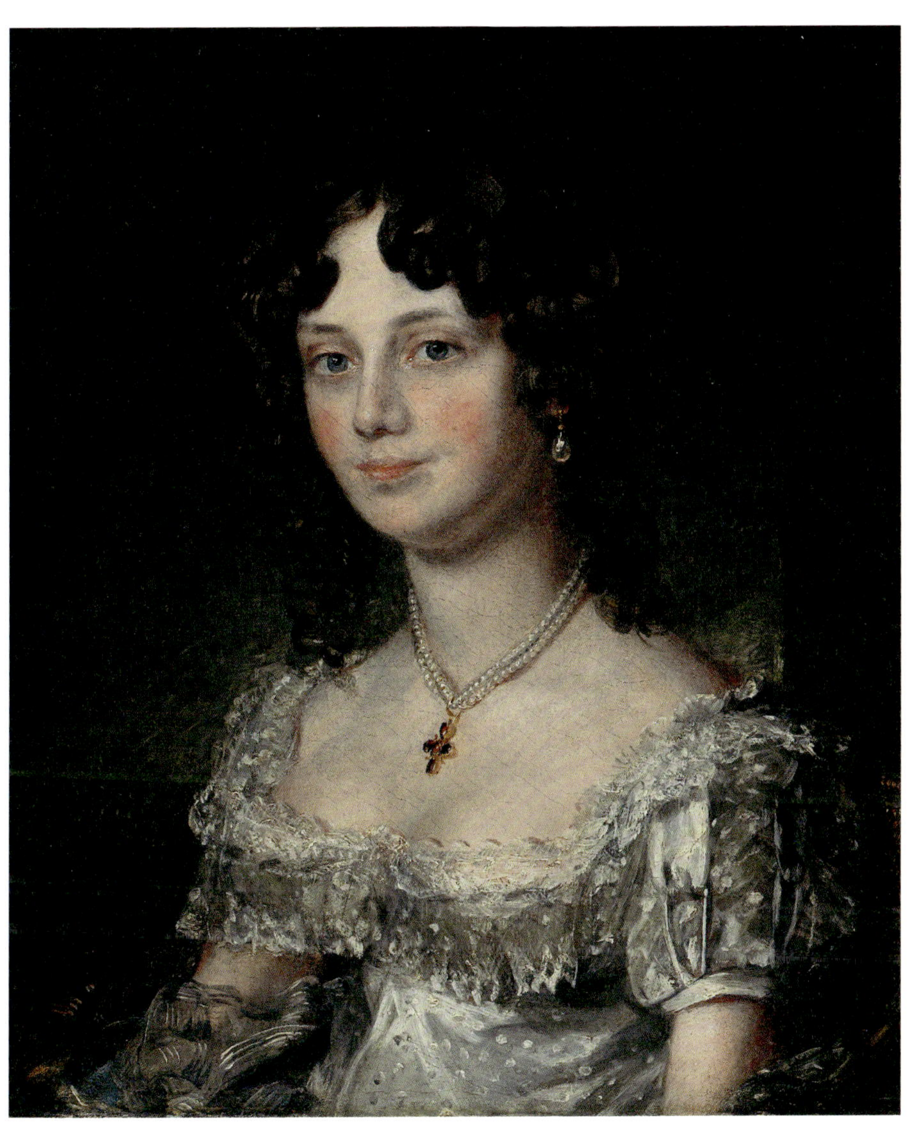

Mrs Mary Fisher
1816
Oil paint on canvas
36 × 30.6

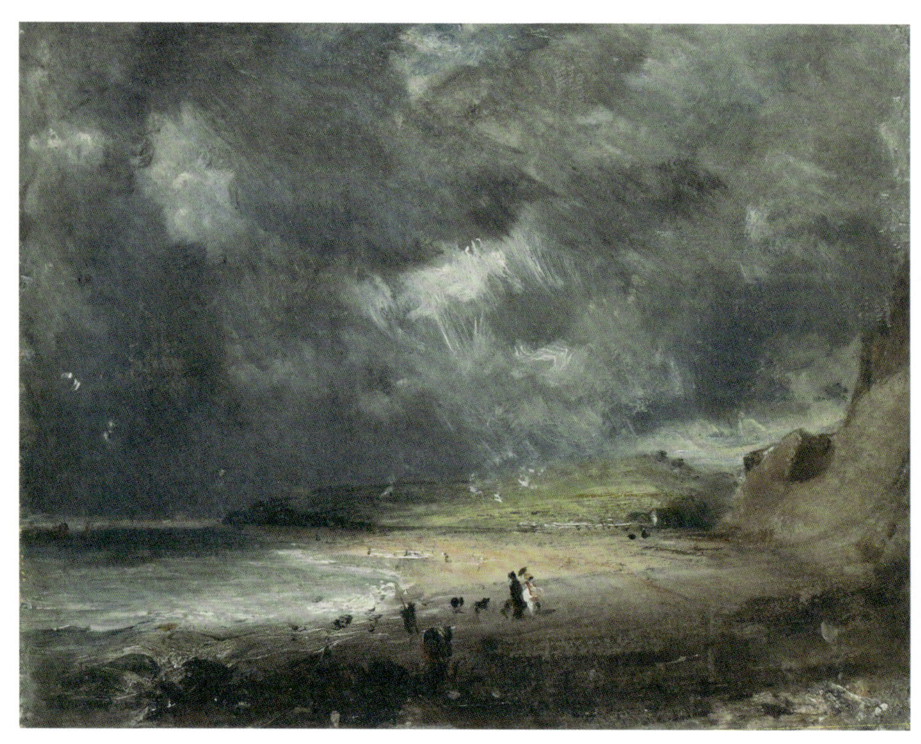

Weymouth Bay (Bowleaze Cove)
1816
Oil paint on board
203 × 247

Weymouth Bay (Bowleaze Cove)
and Jordon Hill 1816
Oil paint on canvas
530 × 750

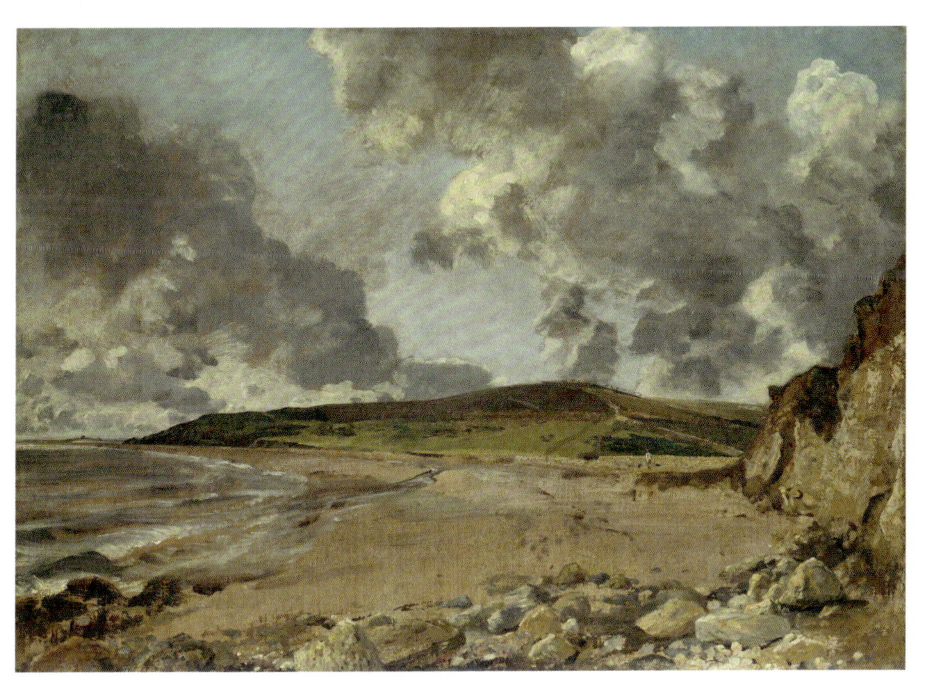

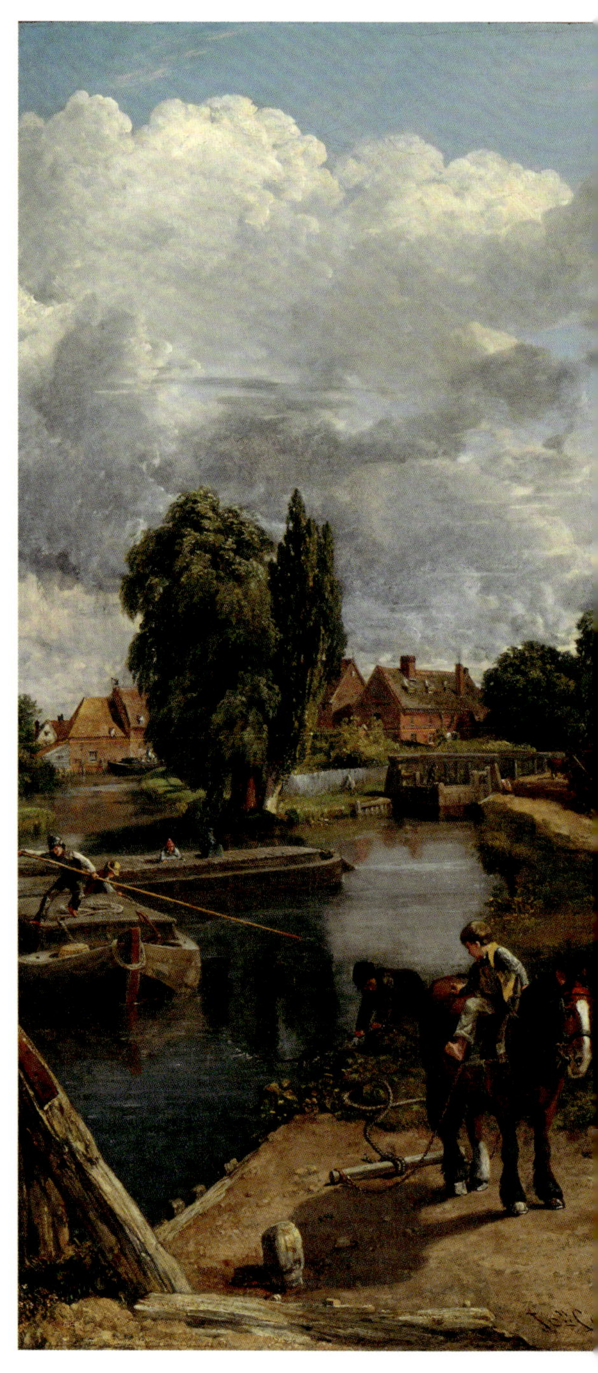

Flatford Mill
('*Scene on a Navigable River*')
1816–17
Oil paint on canvas
101.6 × 127

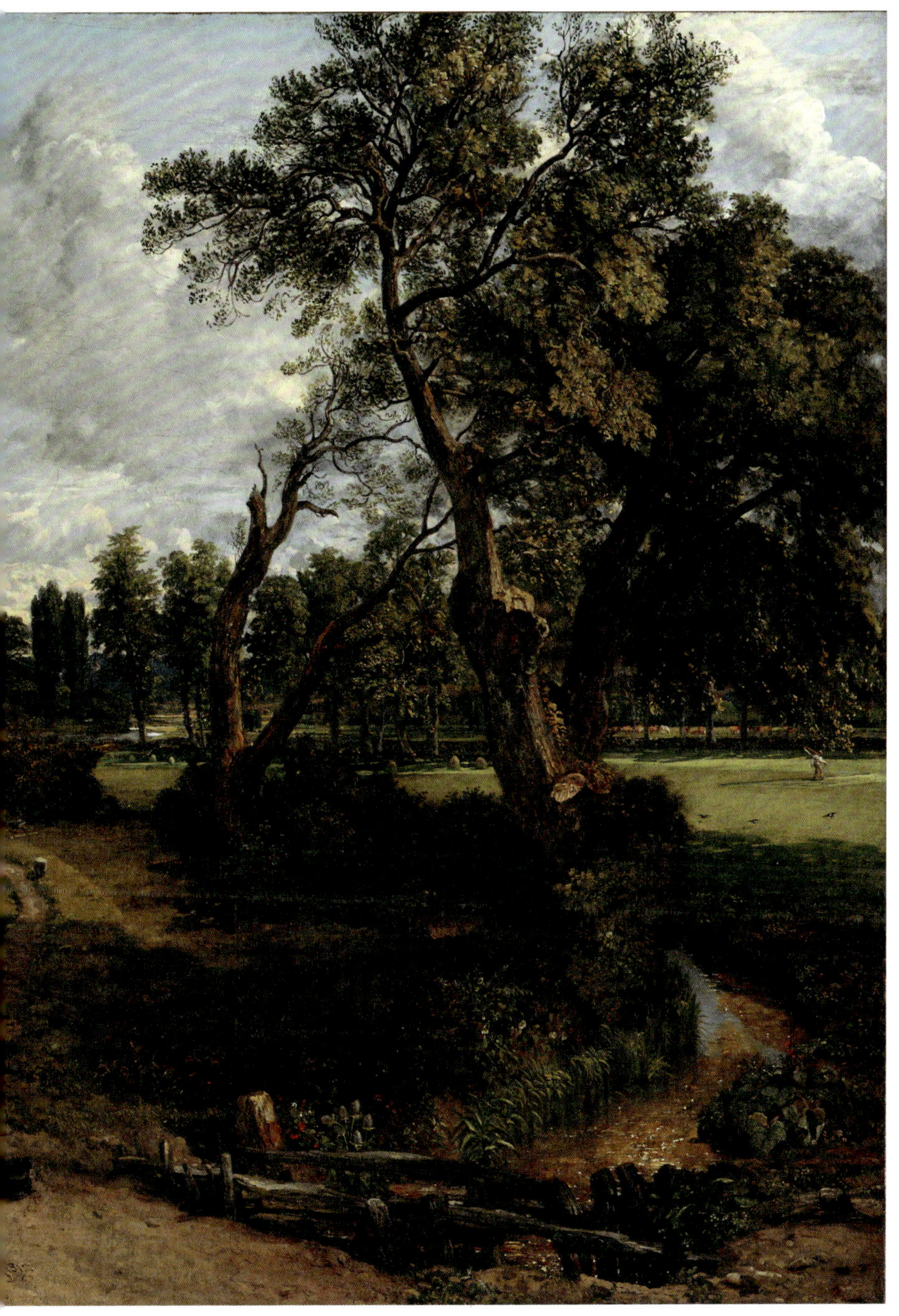

Approach to a Lane,
East Bergholt
29 July 1817
Graphite on paper
11.5 × 18.6

Fen Lane, East Bergholt
?1817
Oil paint on canvas
69.2 × 92.5

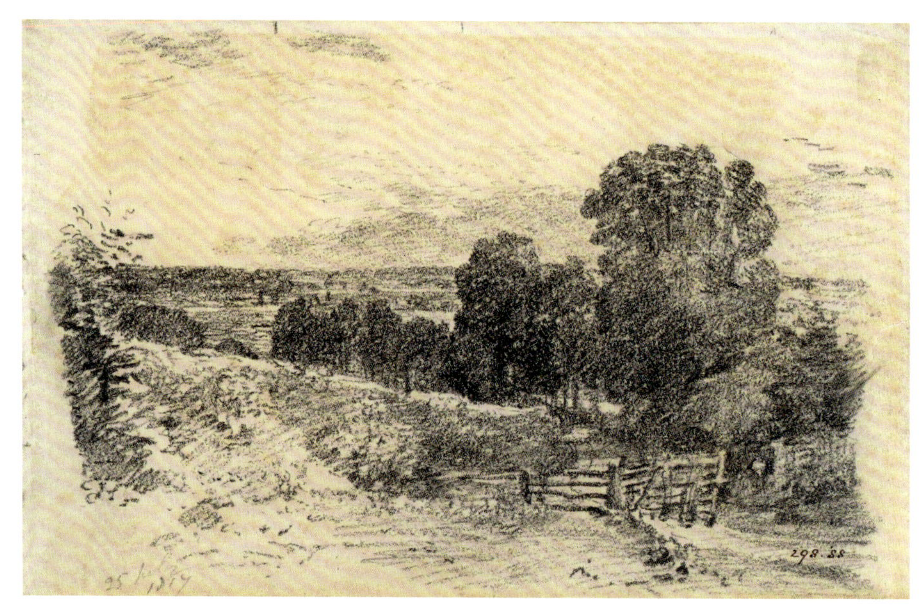

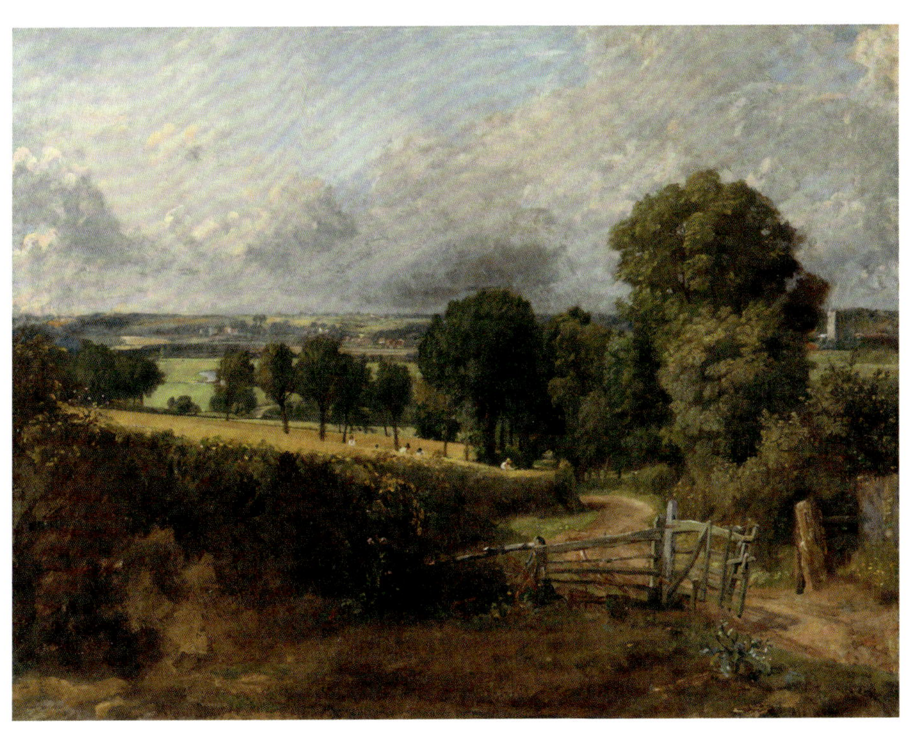

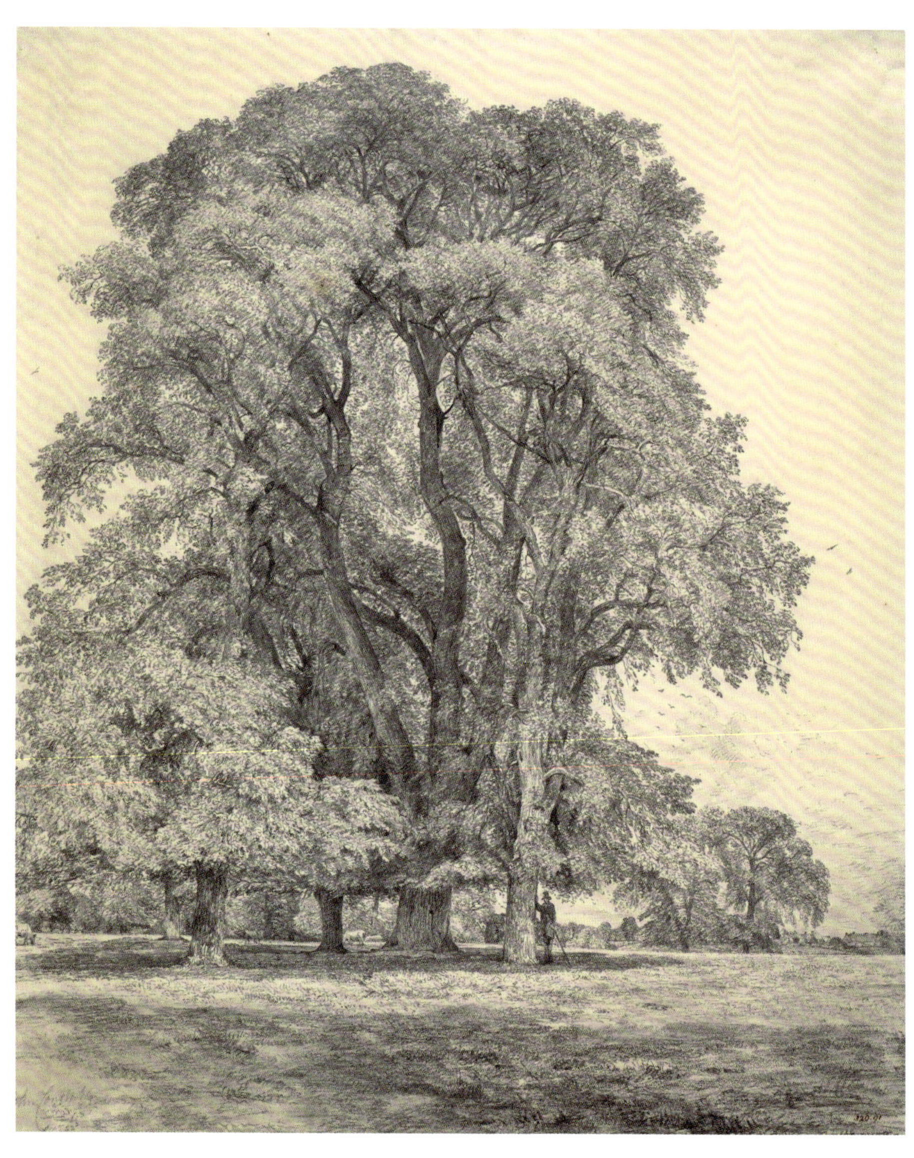

Elm Trees in Old Hall Park,
East Bergholt 1817,
exh.1818
Pencil, grey wash and
gouache on paper
59.1 × 49.5

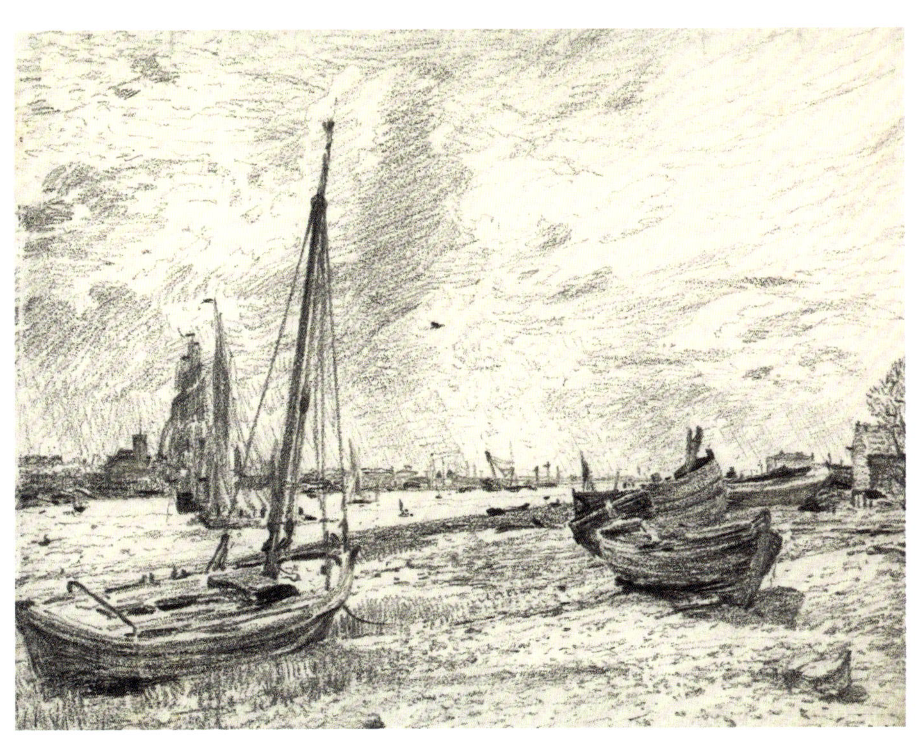

Shipping on the Thames
c.1818
Graphite on paper
9.8 × 13

OVERLEAF
Dedham Lock and Mill
1820
Oil paint on canvas
53.7 × 76.2

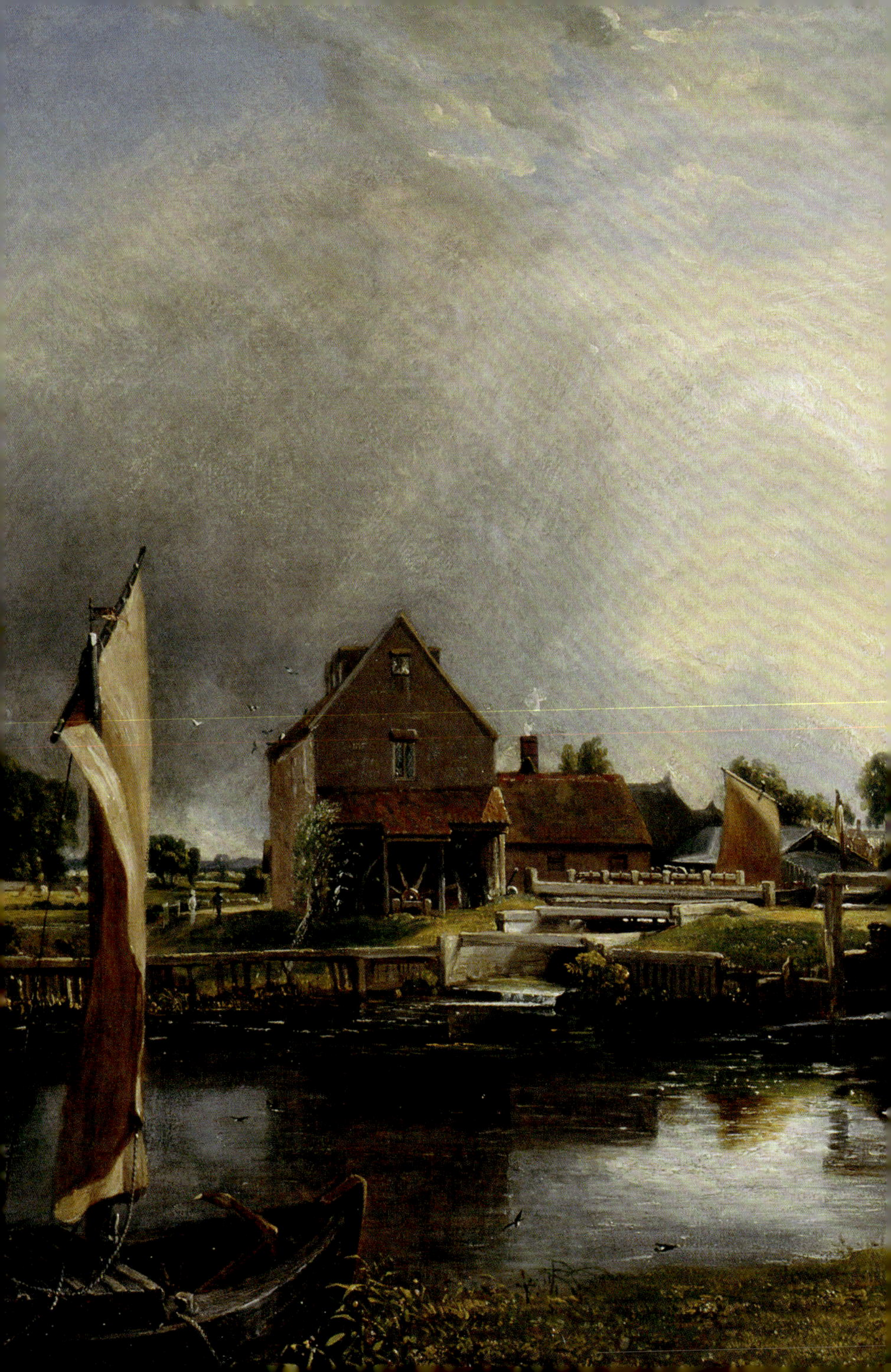

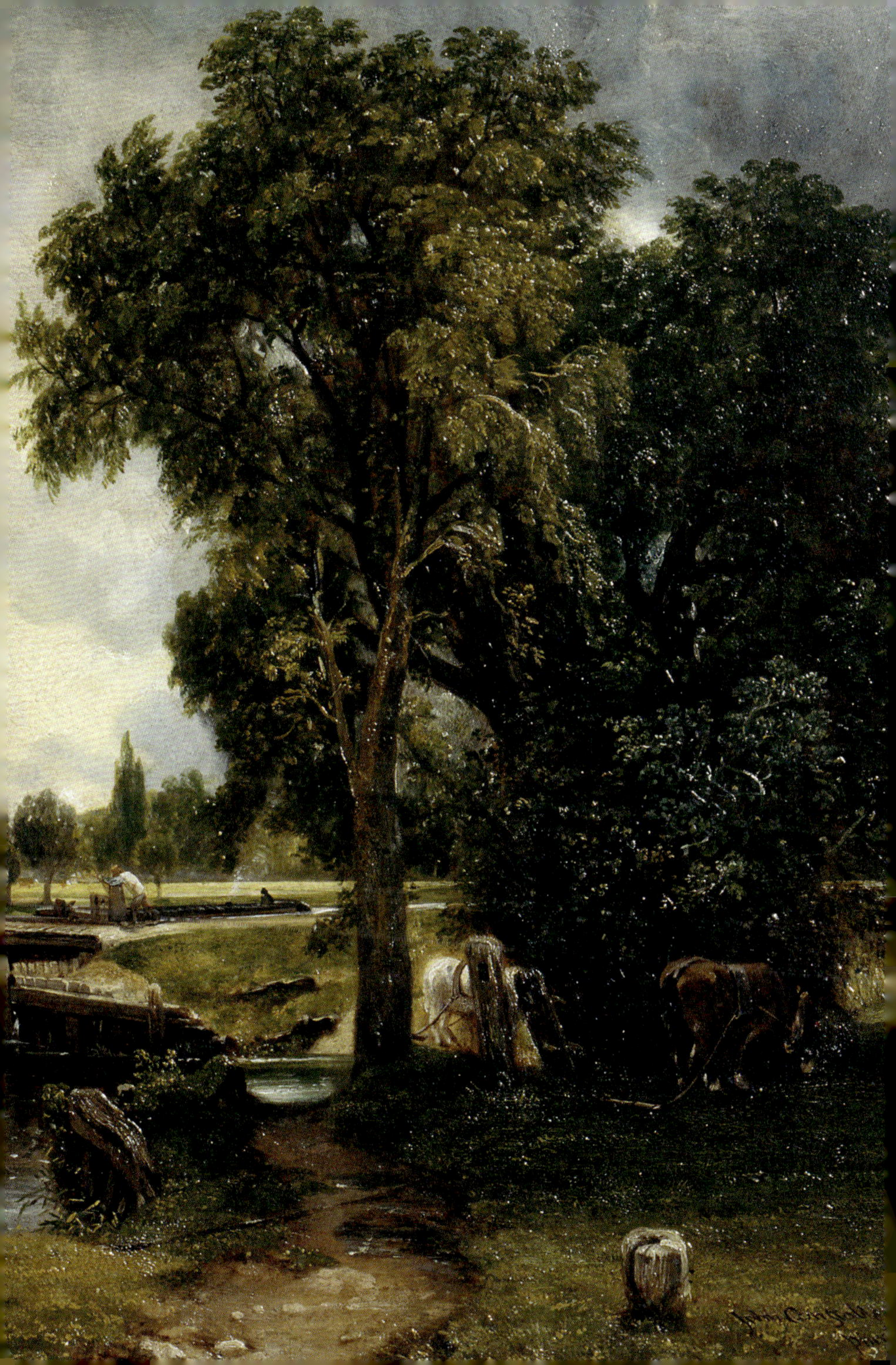

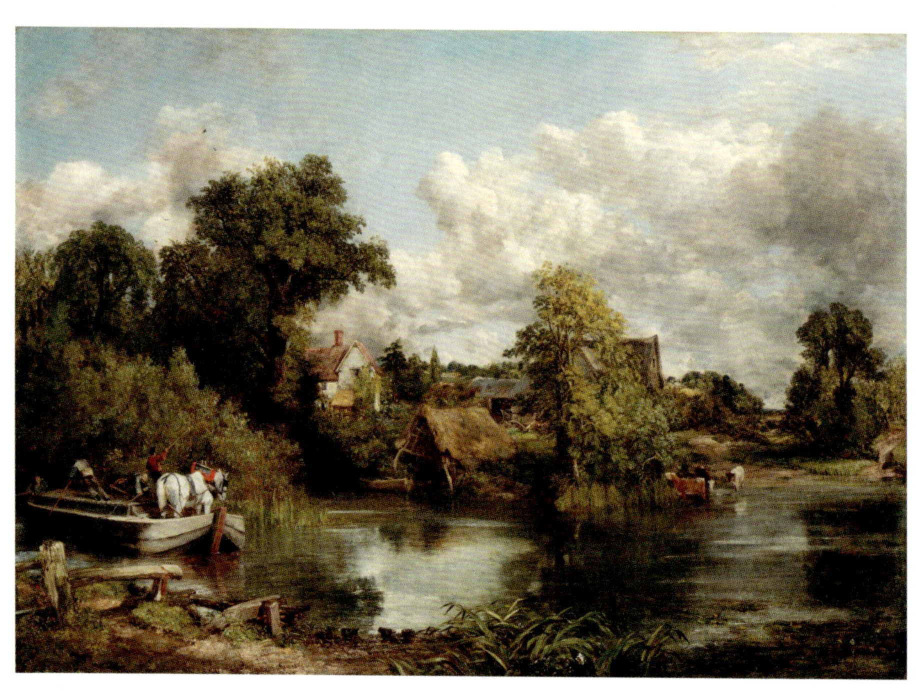

The White Horse
exh.1819
Oil paint on canvas
131.4 × 188.3

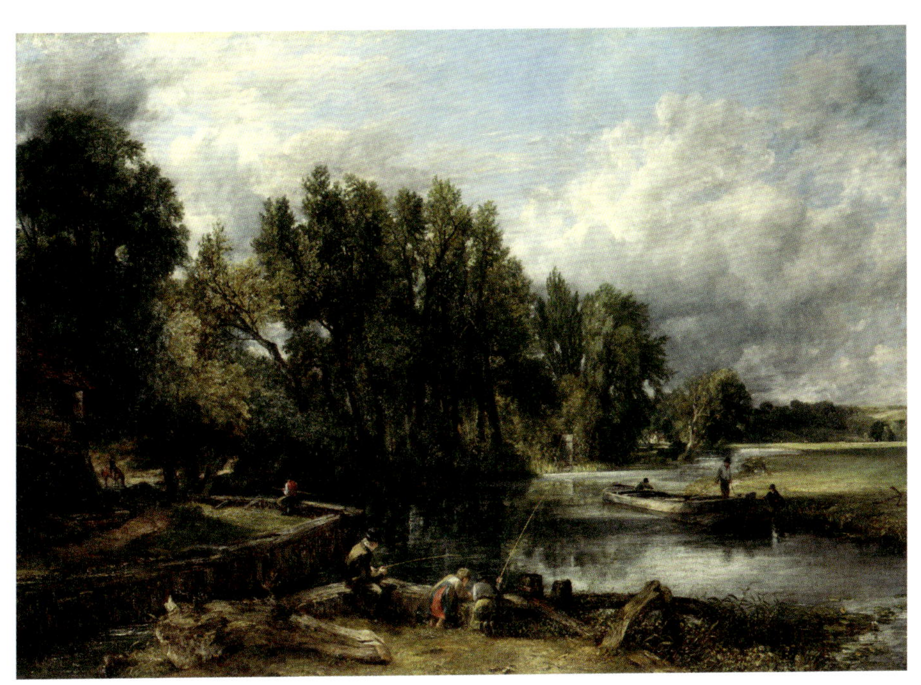

Stratford Mill 1819–20,
exh.1820
Oil paint on canvas
127 × 182.9

Cloud Study 1821
Oil paint on paper on panel
21.3 × 29.2

OPPOSITE
Cloud Study 1821
Oil paint on paper on board
24.8 × 30.2

Cloud Study 1822
Oil paint on paper
30.5 × 49

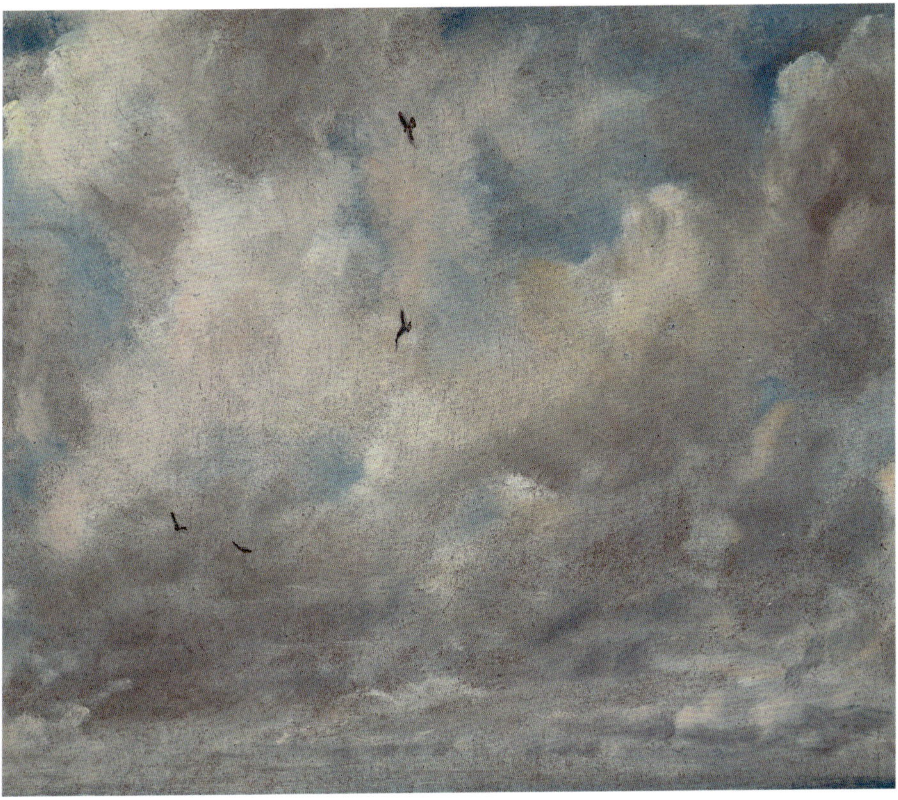

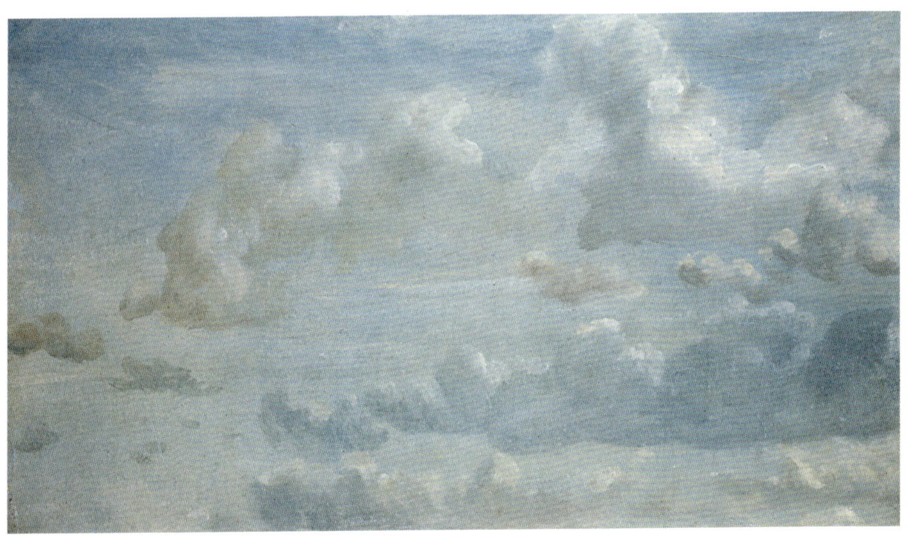

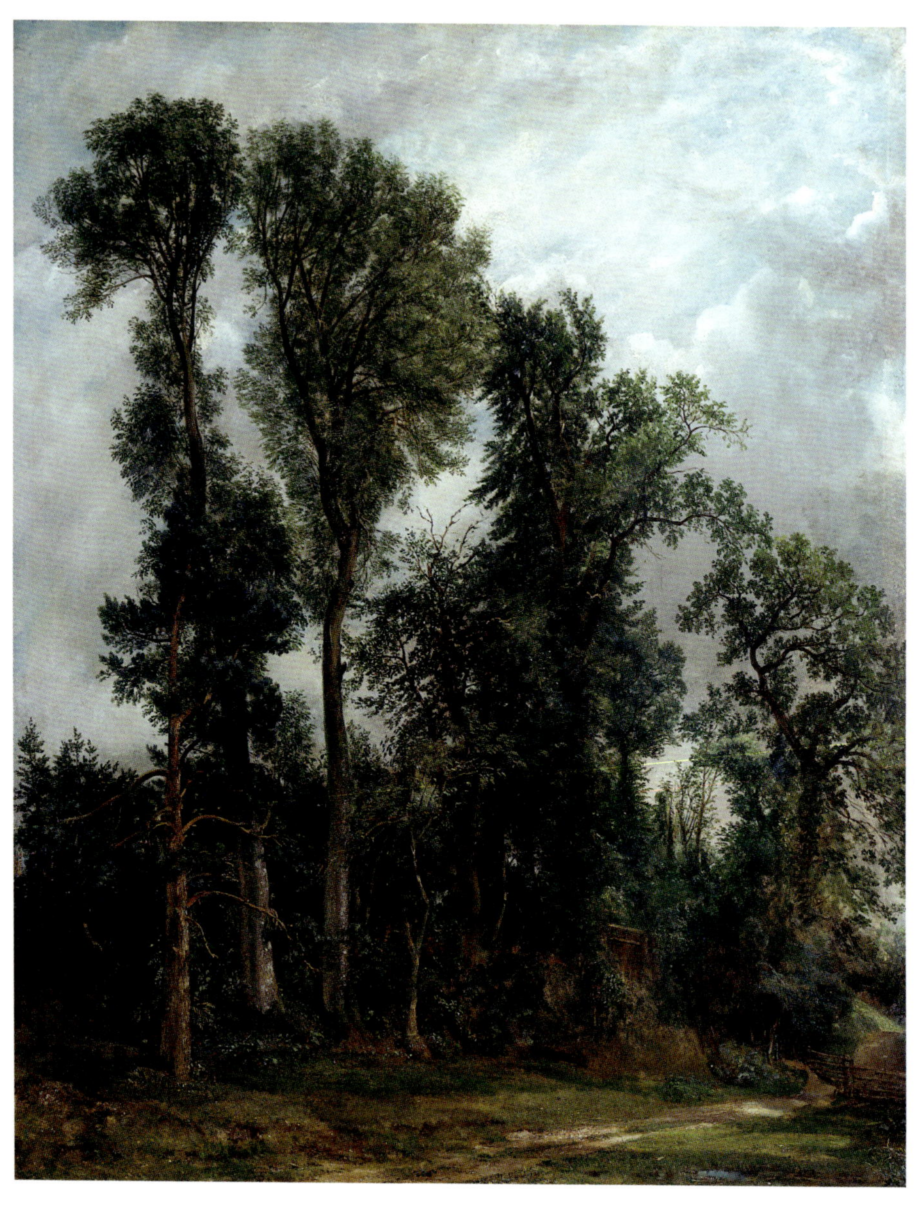

Trees at Hampstead 1821–2,
exh.1822
Oil paint on canvas
91.4 × 72.4

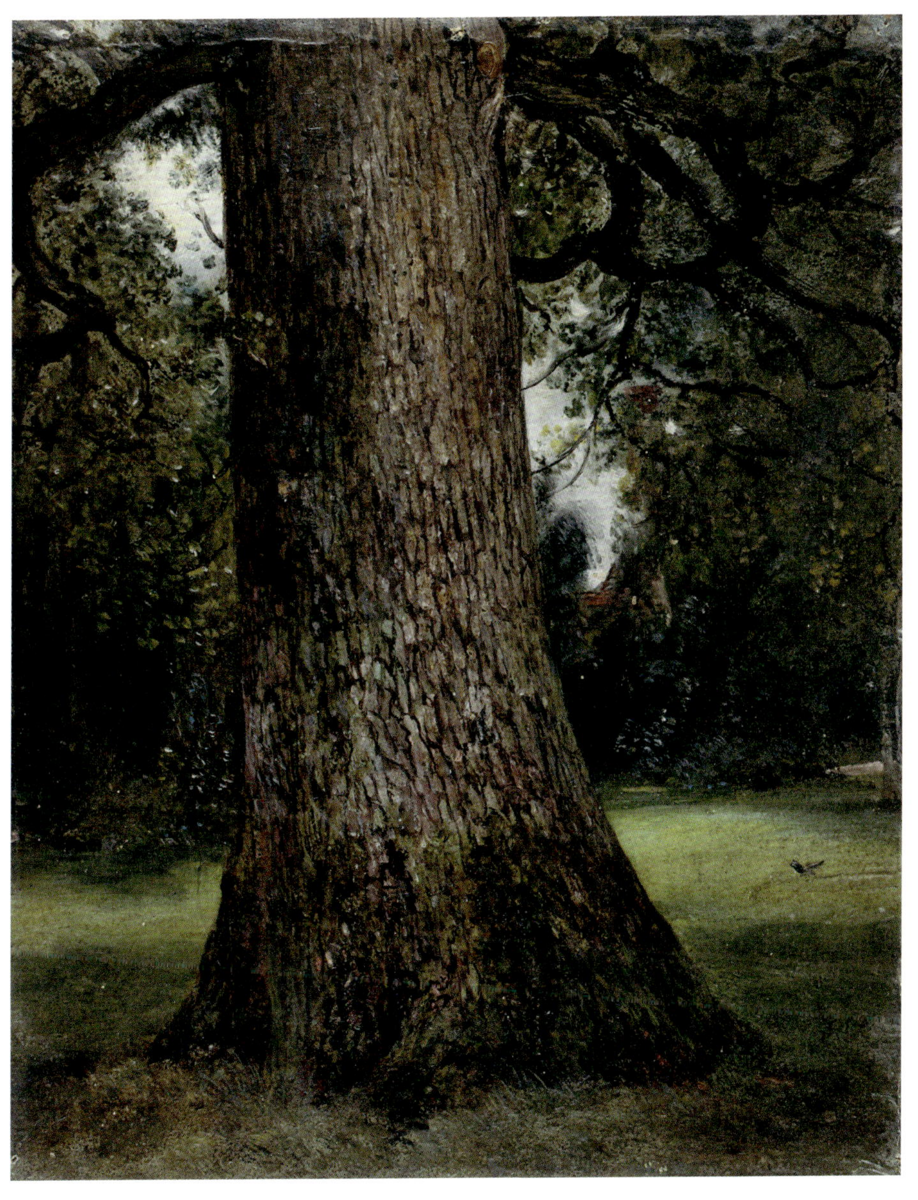

*Study of a Trunk of an Elm
Tree* c.1821
Oil paint on paper
30.6 × 24.8

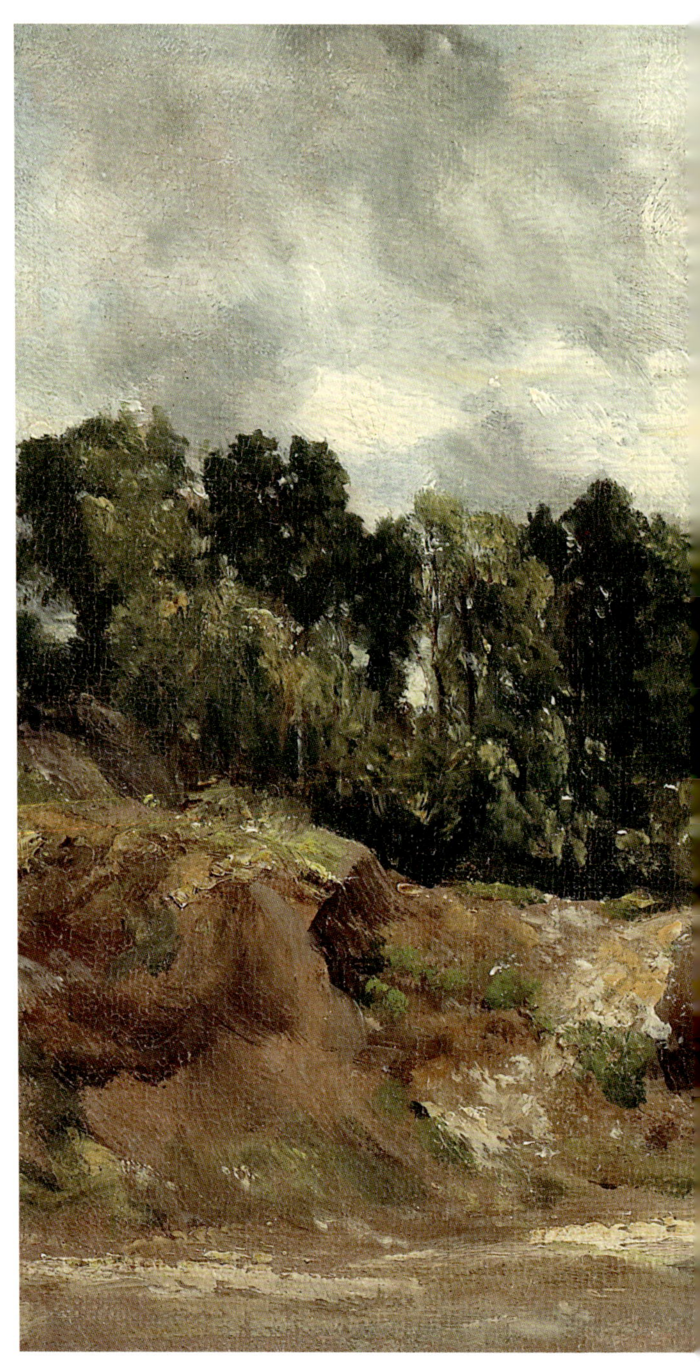

Sandbanks and a Cart and Horses on Hampstead Heath
c.1820–5
Oil paint on canvas
19.7 × 25.4

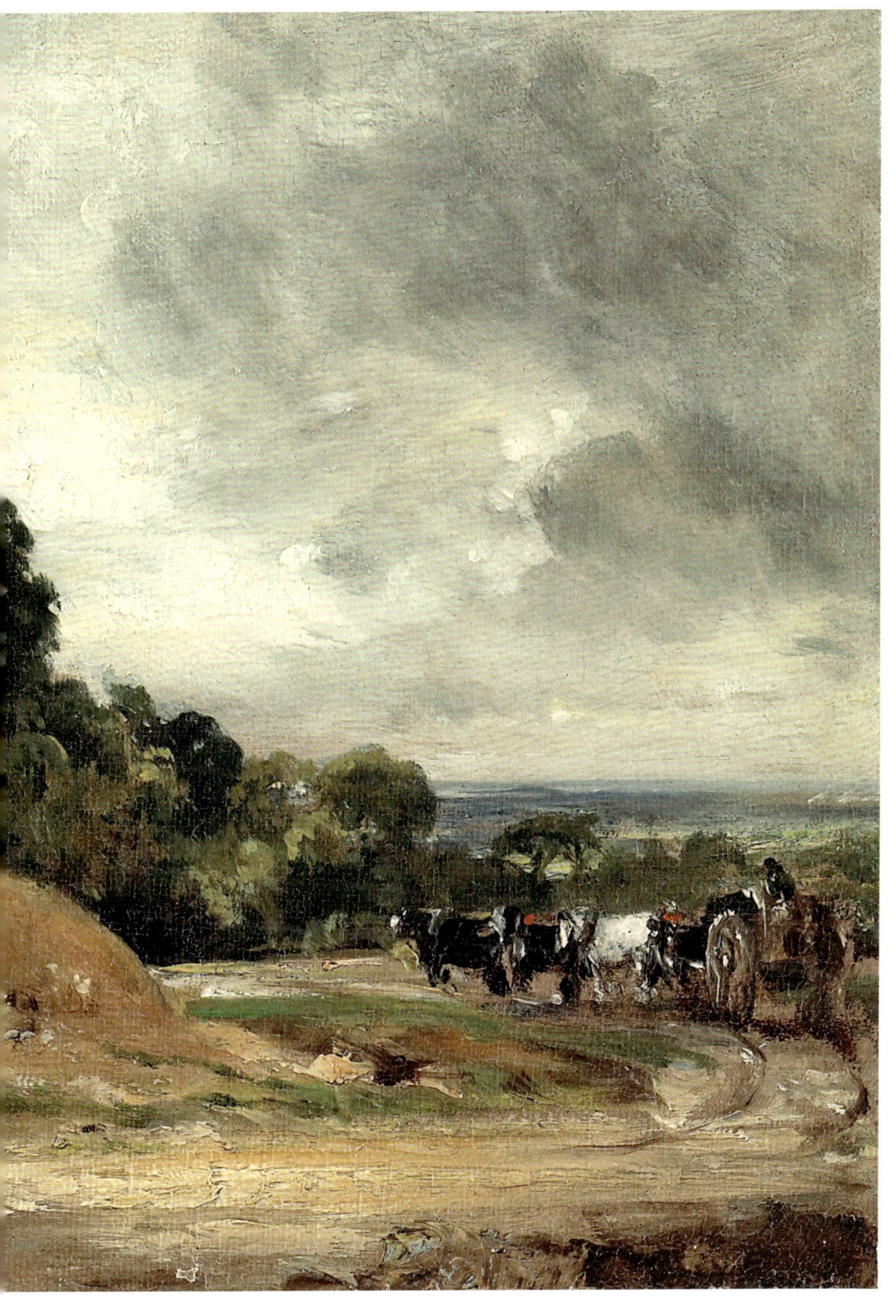

*Salisbury Cathedral from the
Bishop's Grounds* exh.1823
Oil paint on canvas
87.6 × 111.8

Parham Mill, Gillingham 1826,
exh.1826
Oil paint on canvas
50.2 × 60.3

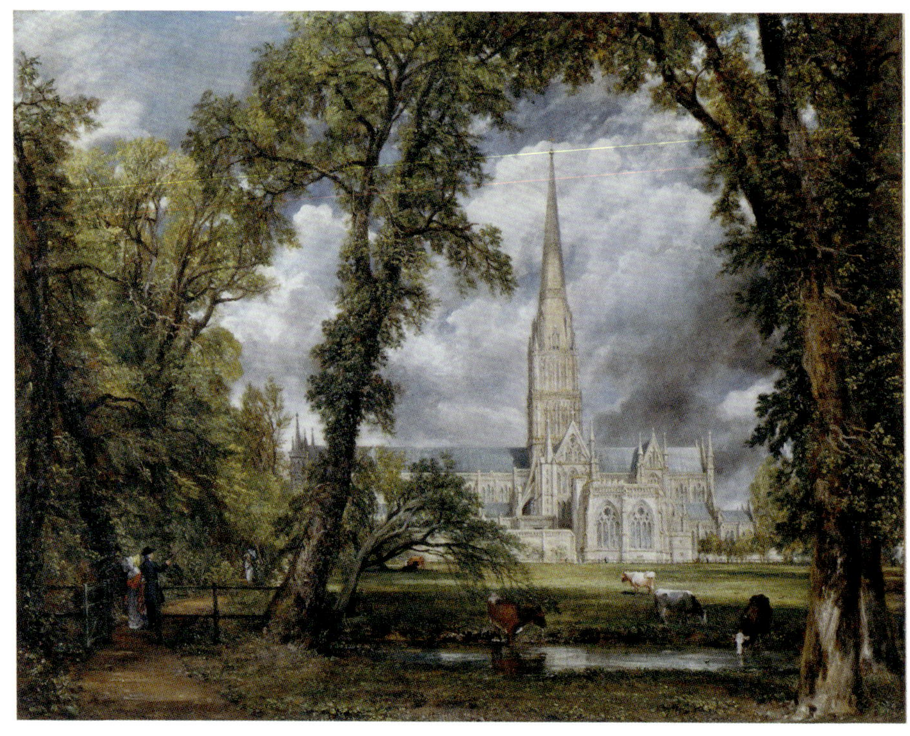

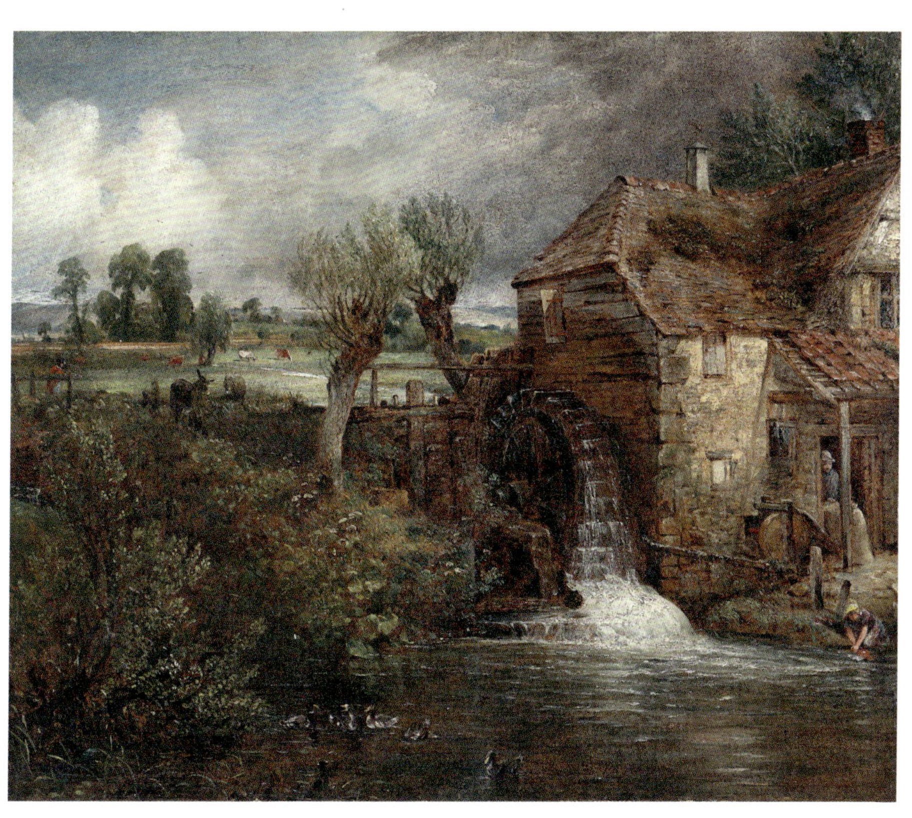

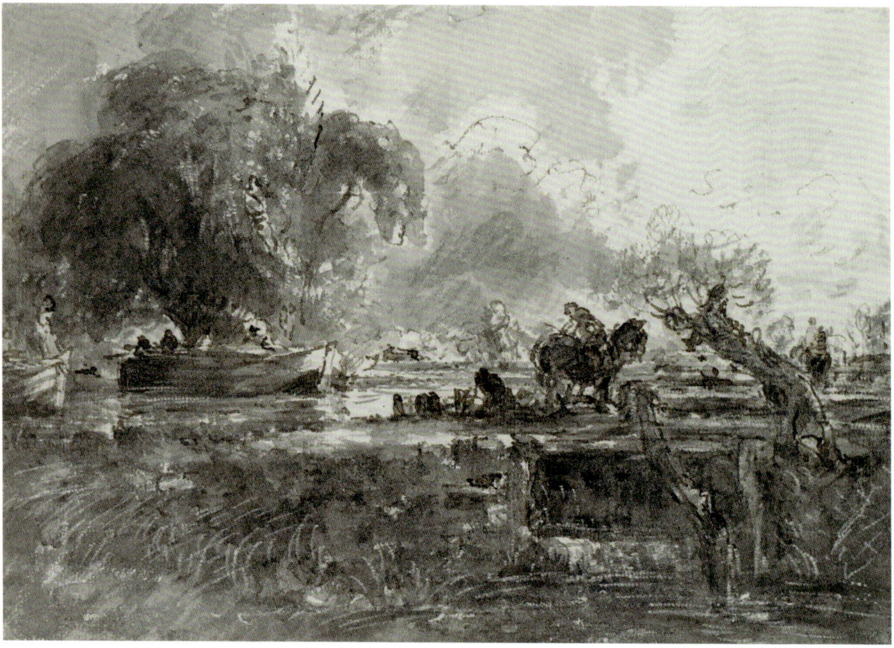

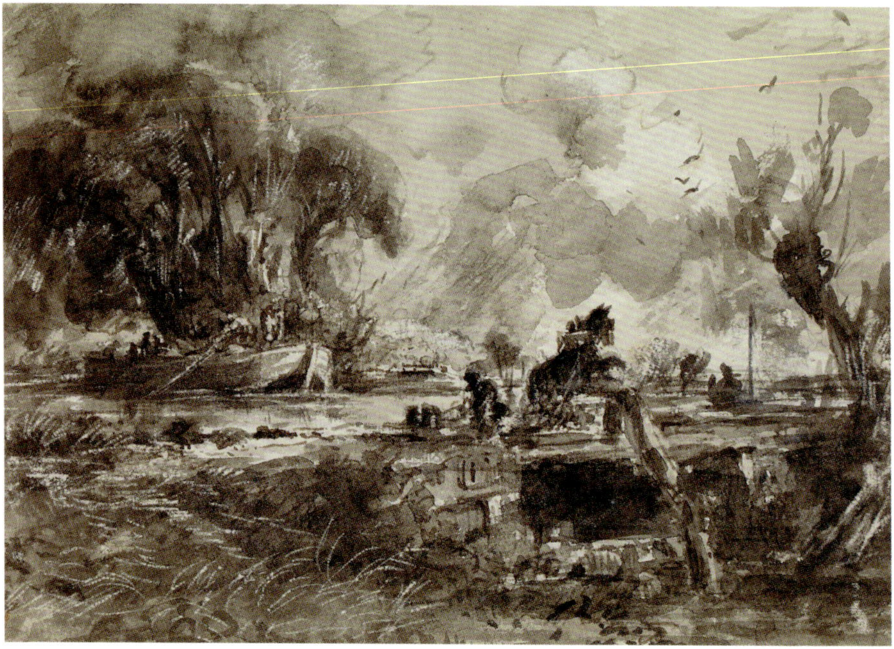

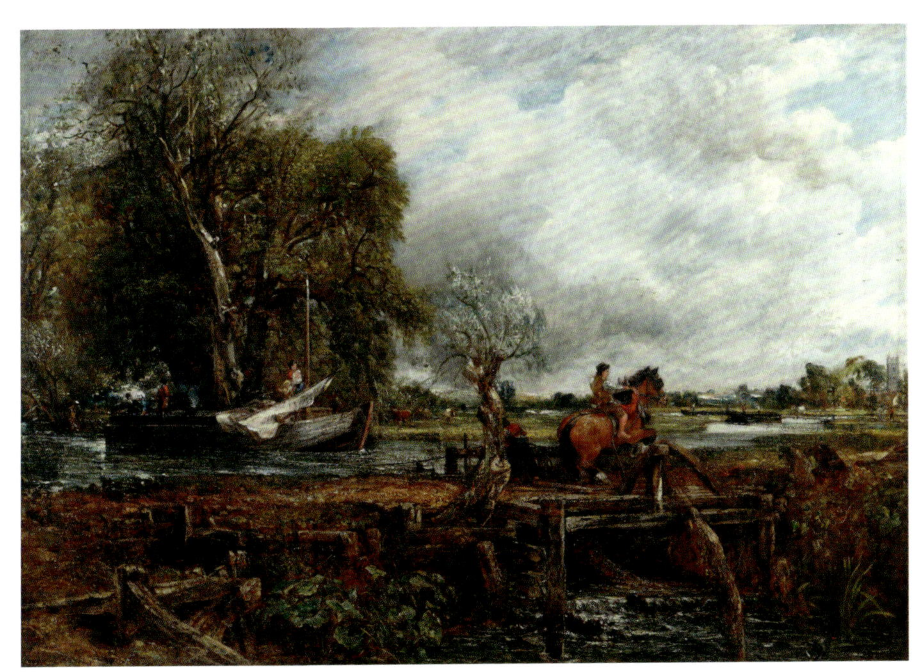

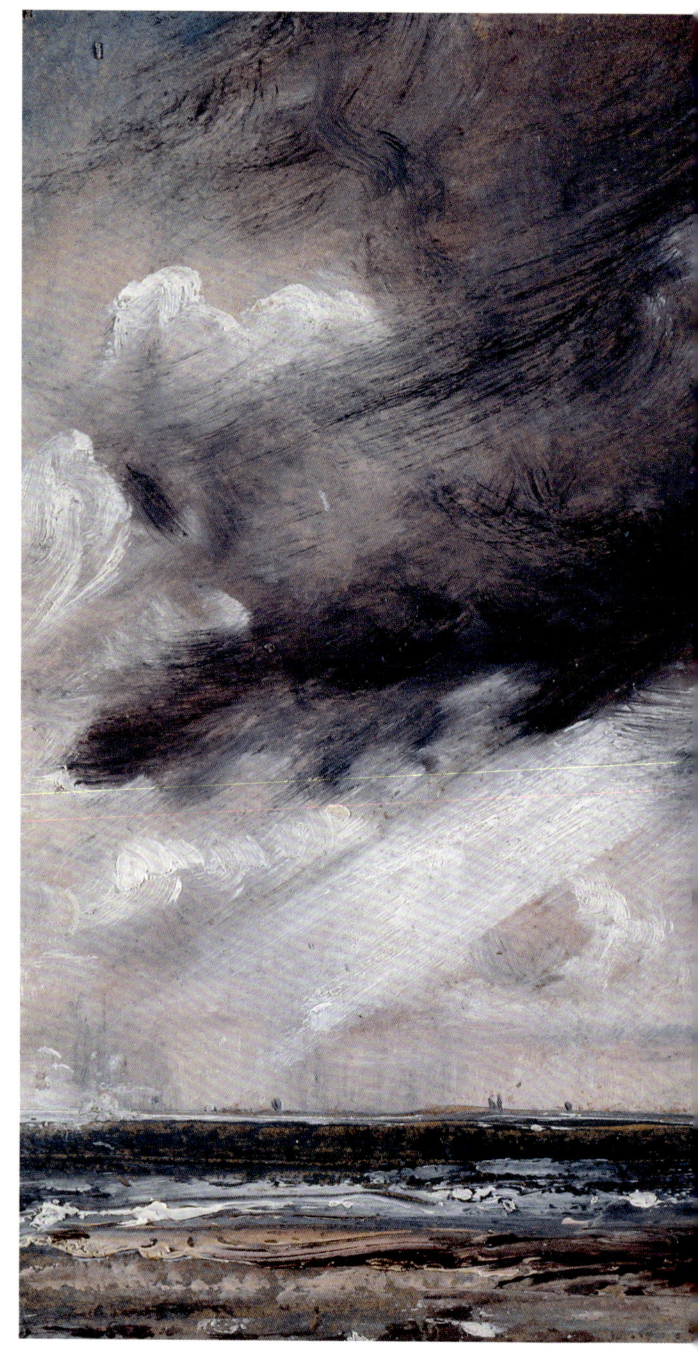

Rainstorm over the Sea
c.1824–8
Oil paint on paper
on canvas
23.5 × 32.6

OVERLEAF
Chain Pier, Brighton 1826–7,
exh.1827
Oil paint on canvas
127 × 182.9

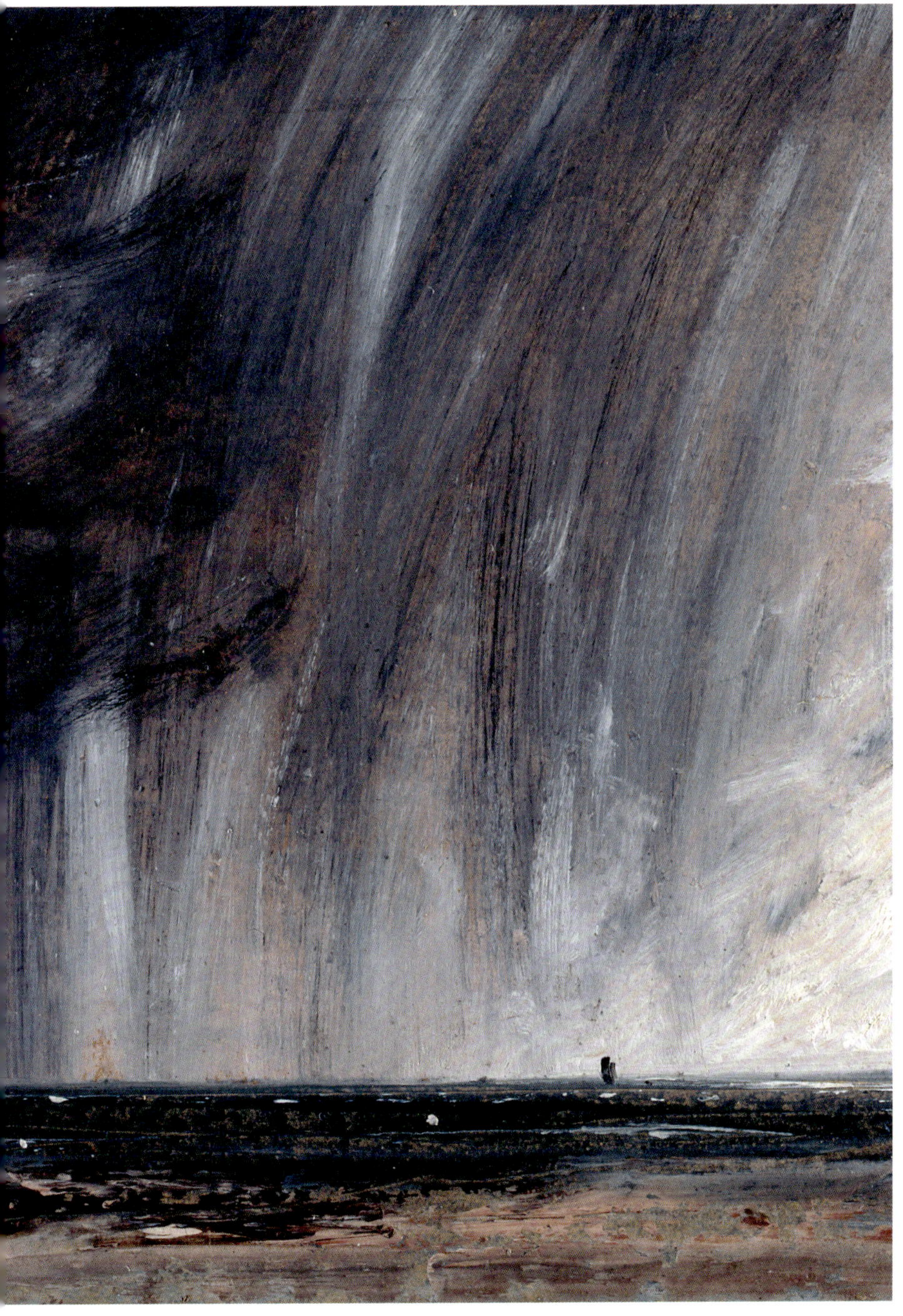

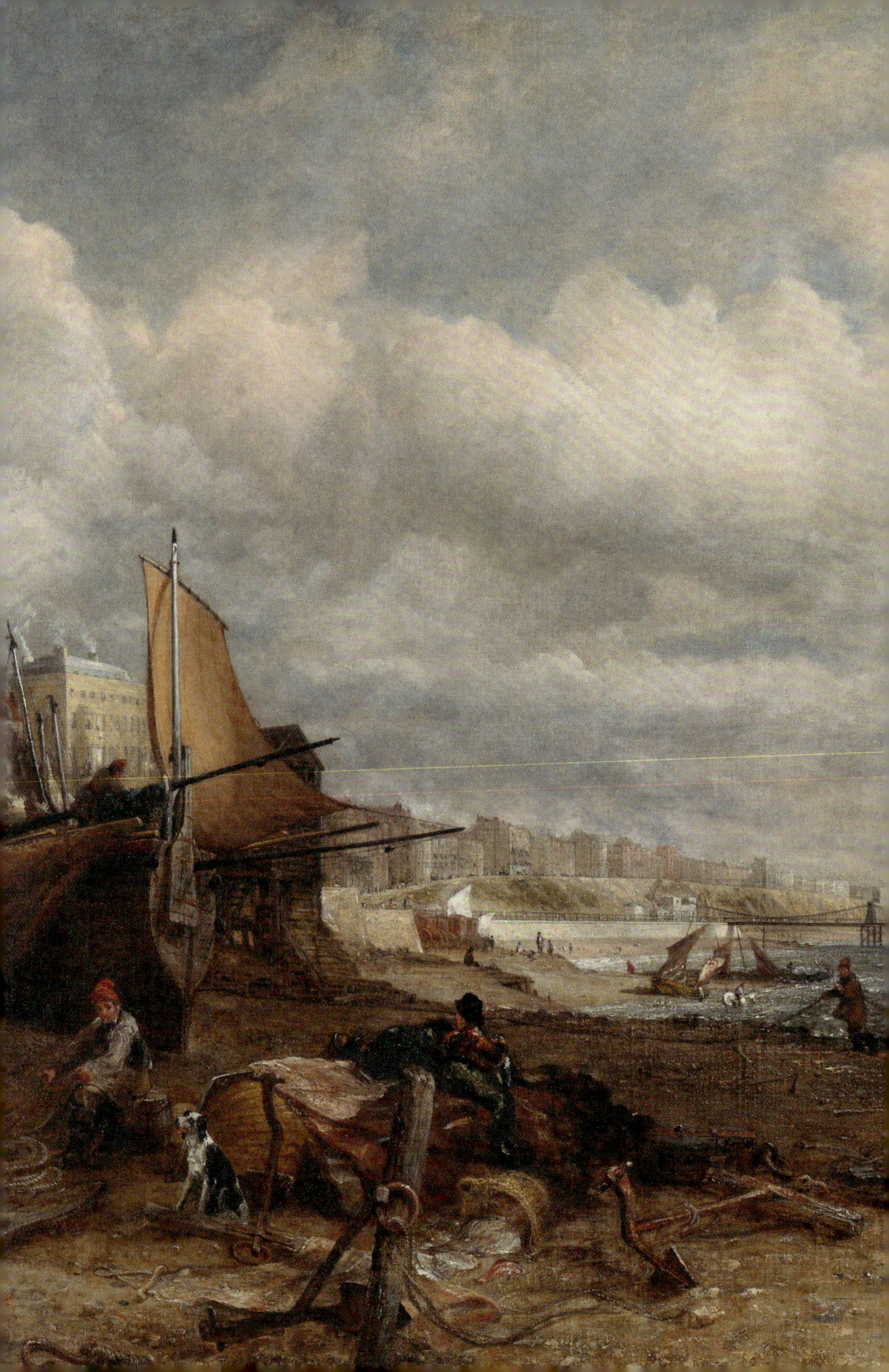

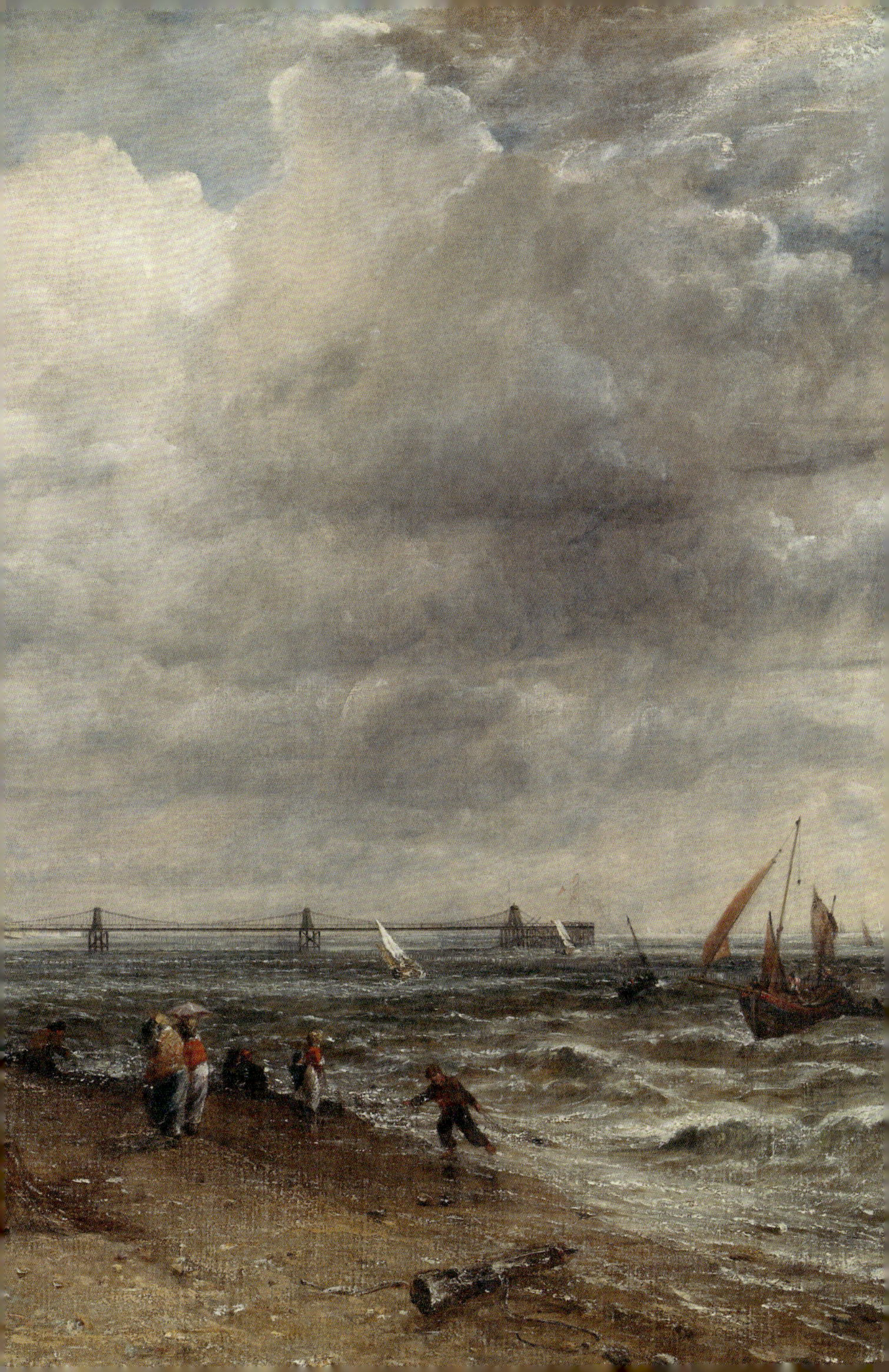

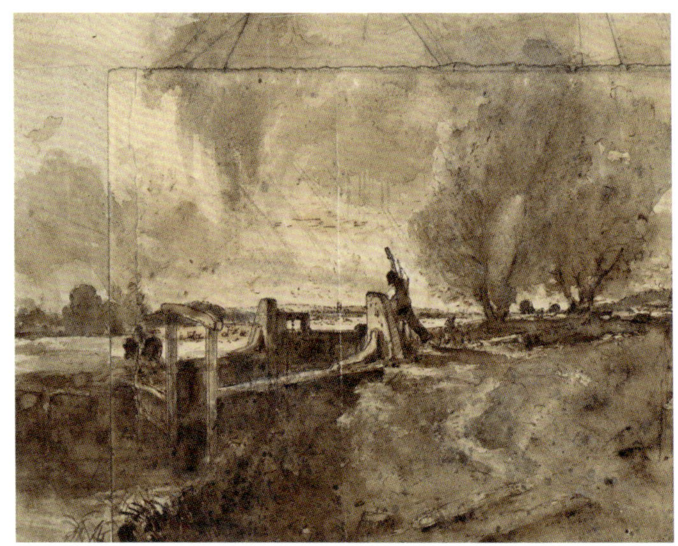

The Lock c.1826
Graphite, wash and
gouache on paper
28.7 × 36.4

A Boat passing a Lock
1826
Oil paint on canvas
101.6 × 127

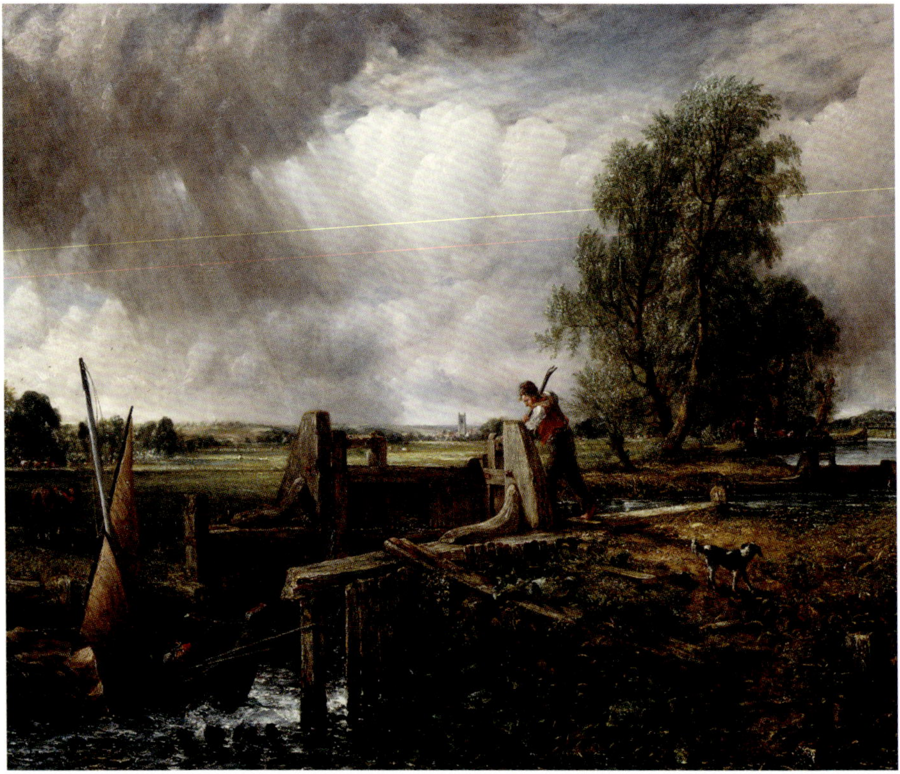

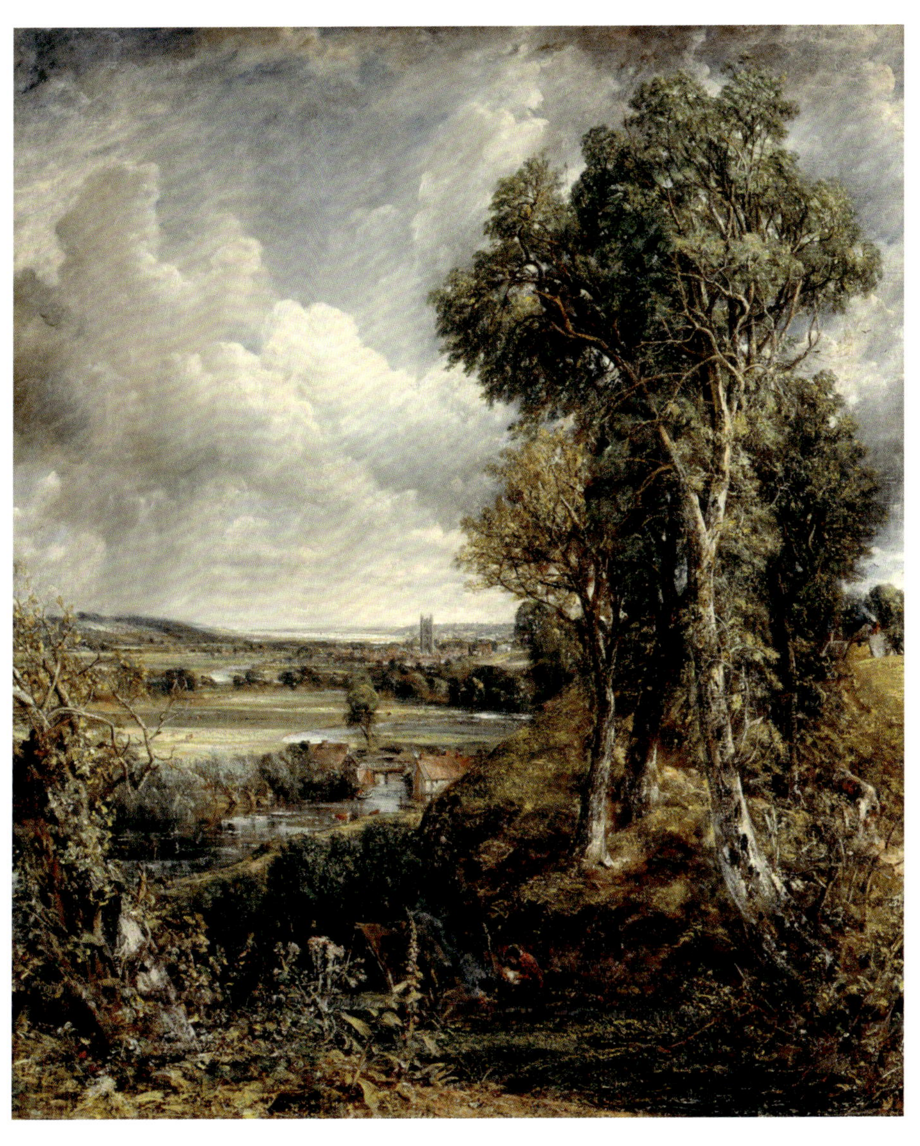

Dedham Vale ?1827–8,
exh.1828
Oil paint on canvas
145 × 122

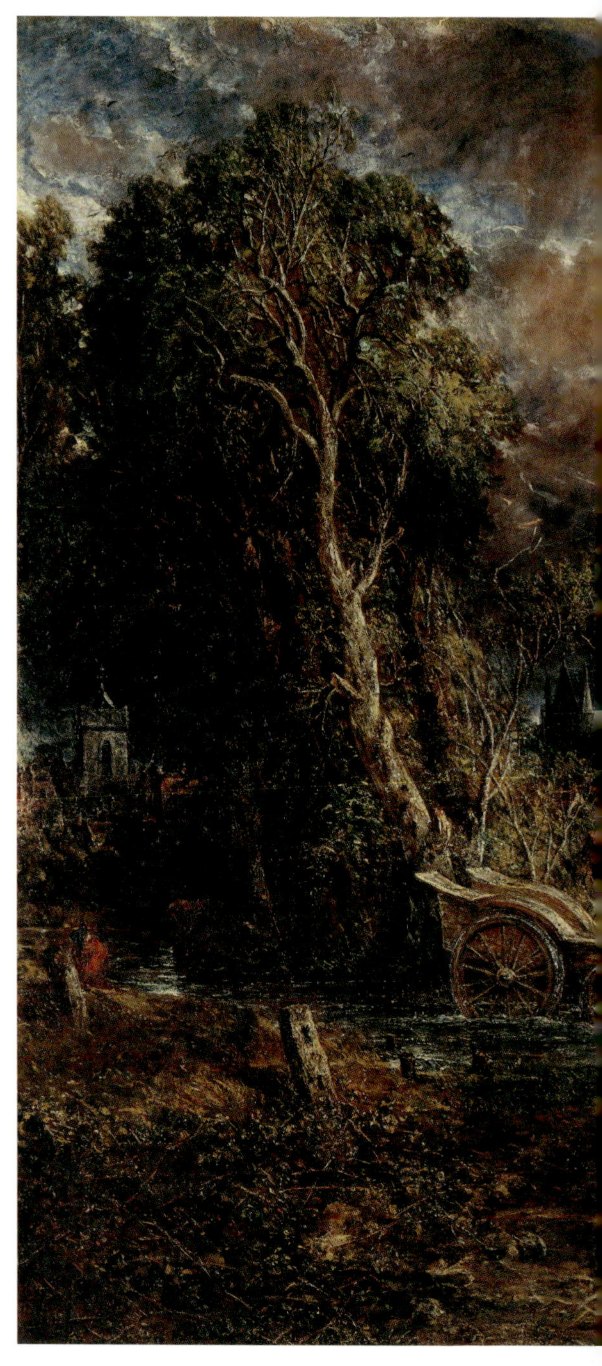

*Salisbury Cathedral from
the Meadows* exh.1831
Oil paint on canvas
153.7 × 192

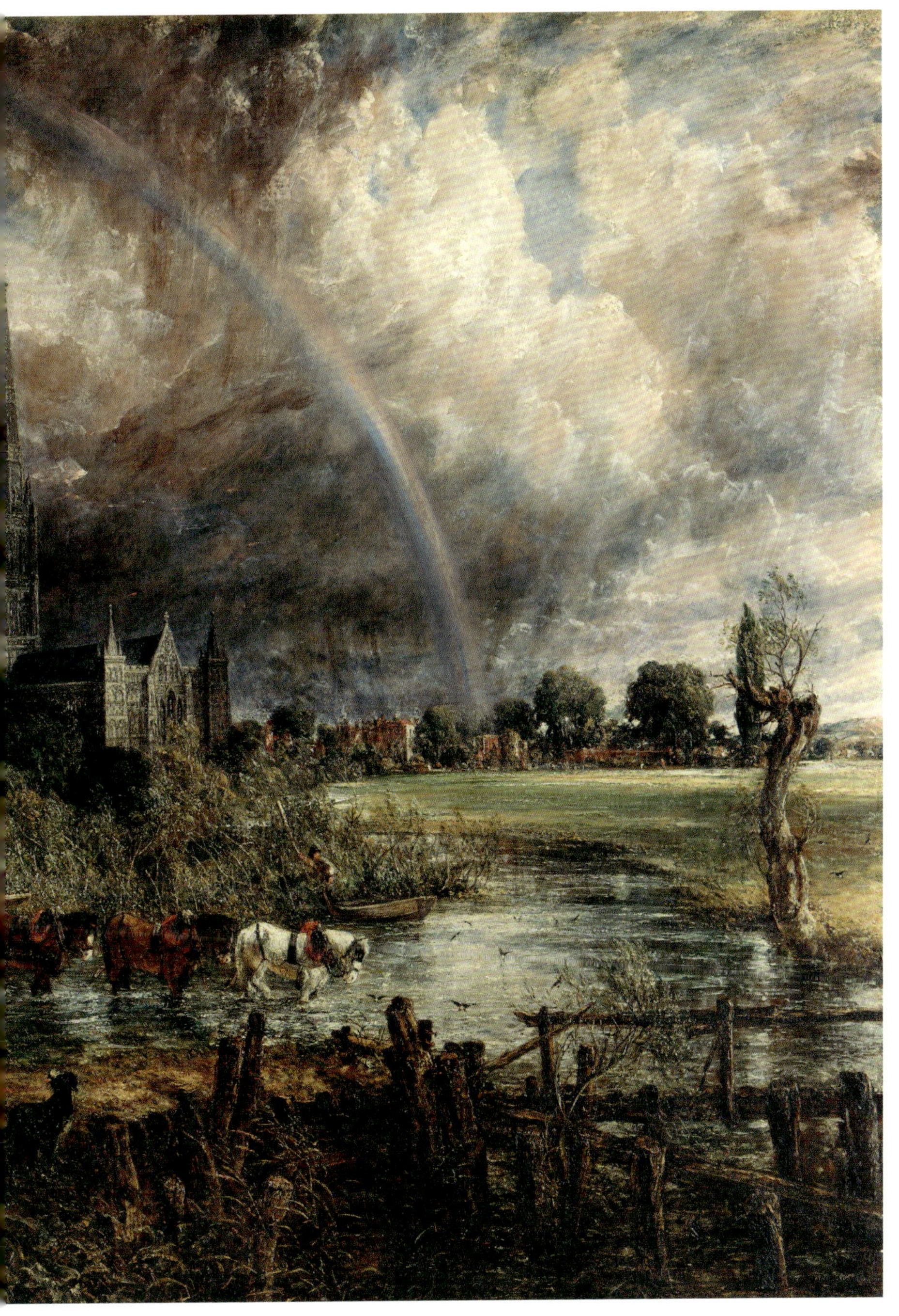

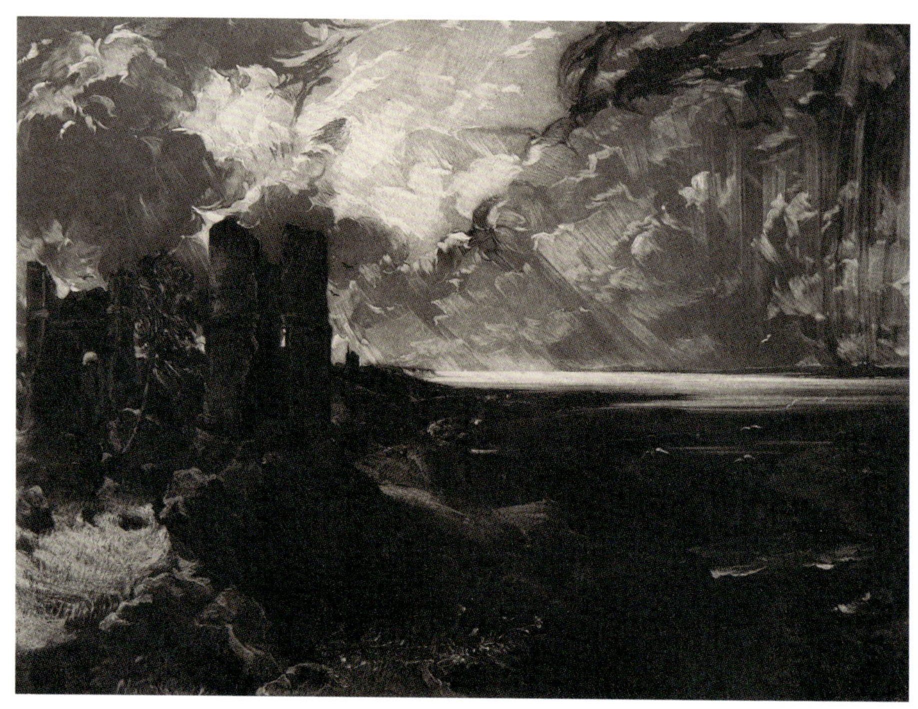

David Lucas after John
Constable *Hadleigh Castle
near the Nore* 1830–2
Mezzotint and etching
on paper
33 × 45.7

*Hadleigh Castle, The Mouth
of the Thames – Morning after
a Stormy Night* exh.1829
Oil paint on canvas
121.9 × 164.5

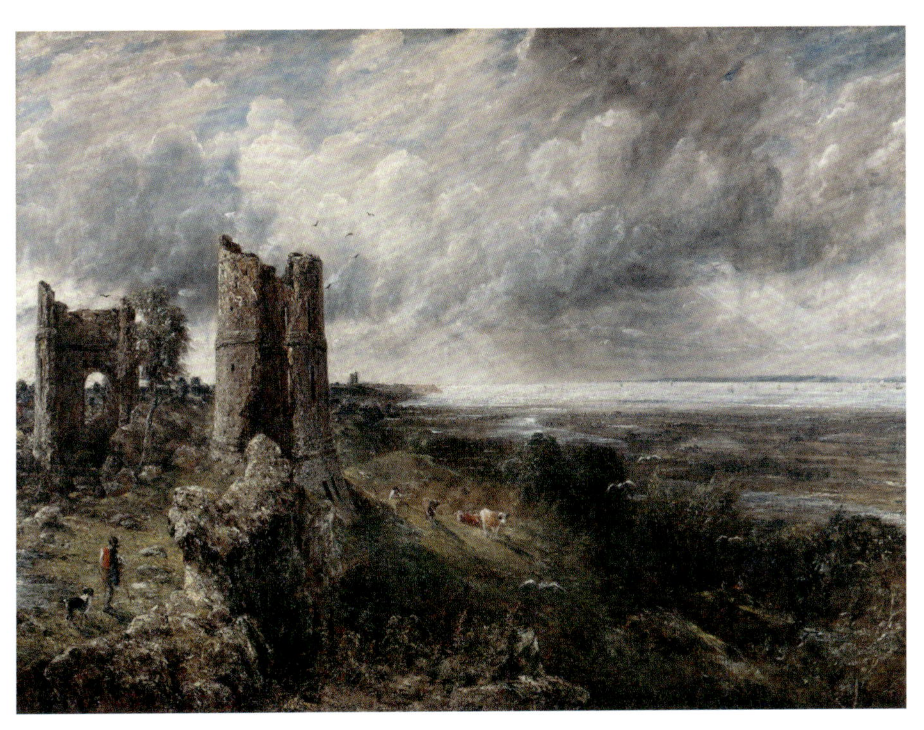

OVERLEAF
The Opening of Waterloo Bridge
('Whitehall Stairs, June 18th,
1817') exh.1832
Oil paint on canvas
130.8 × 218

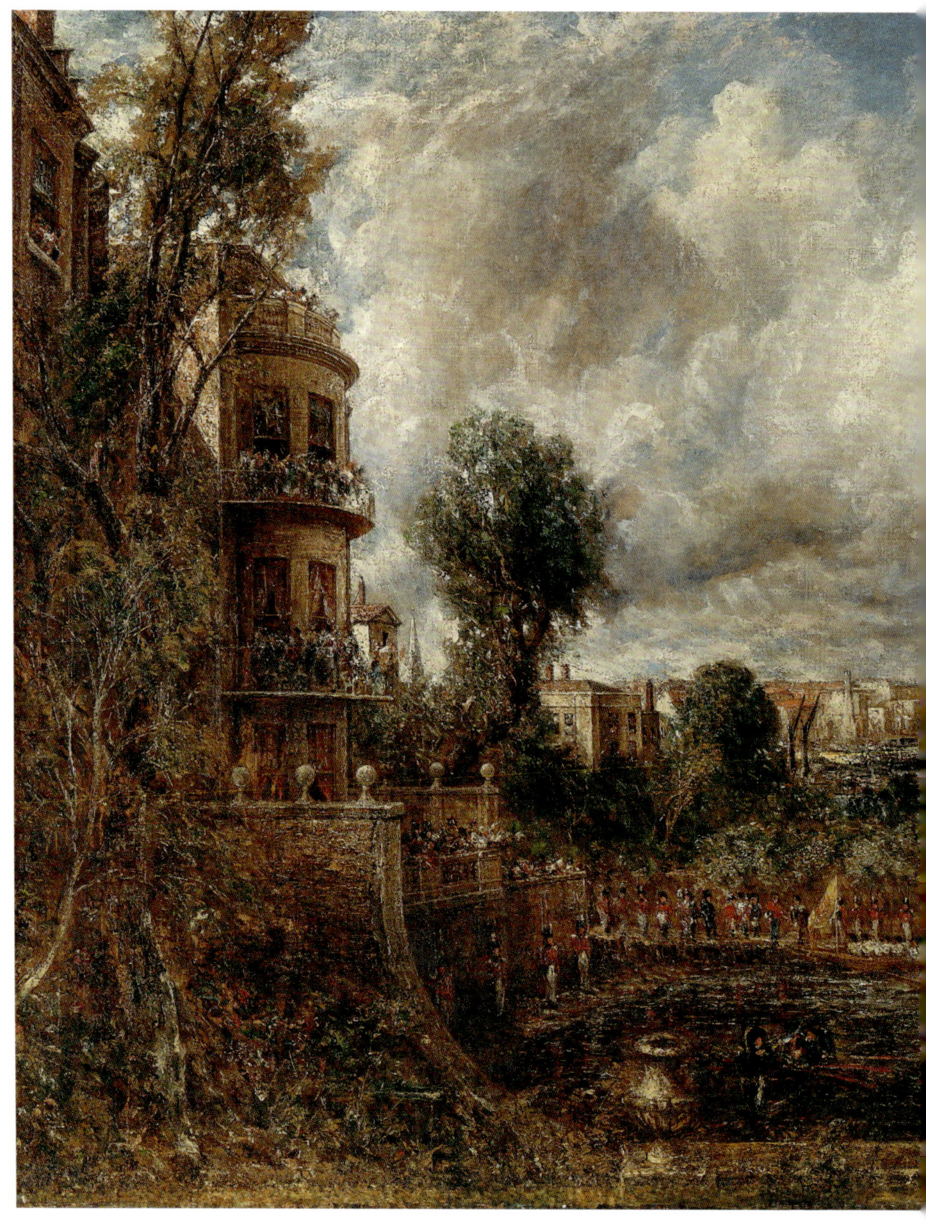

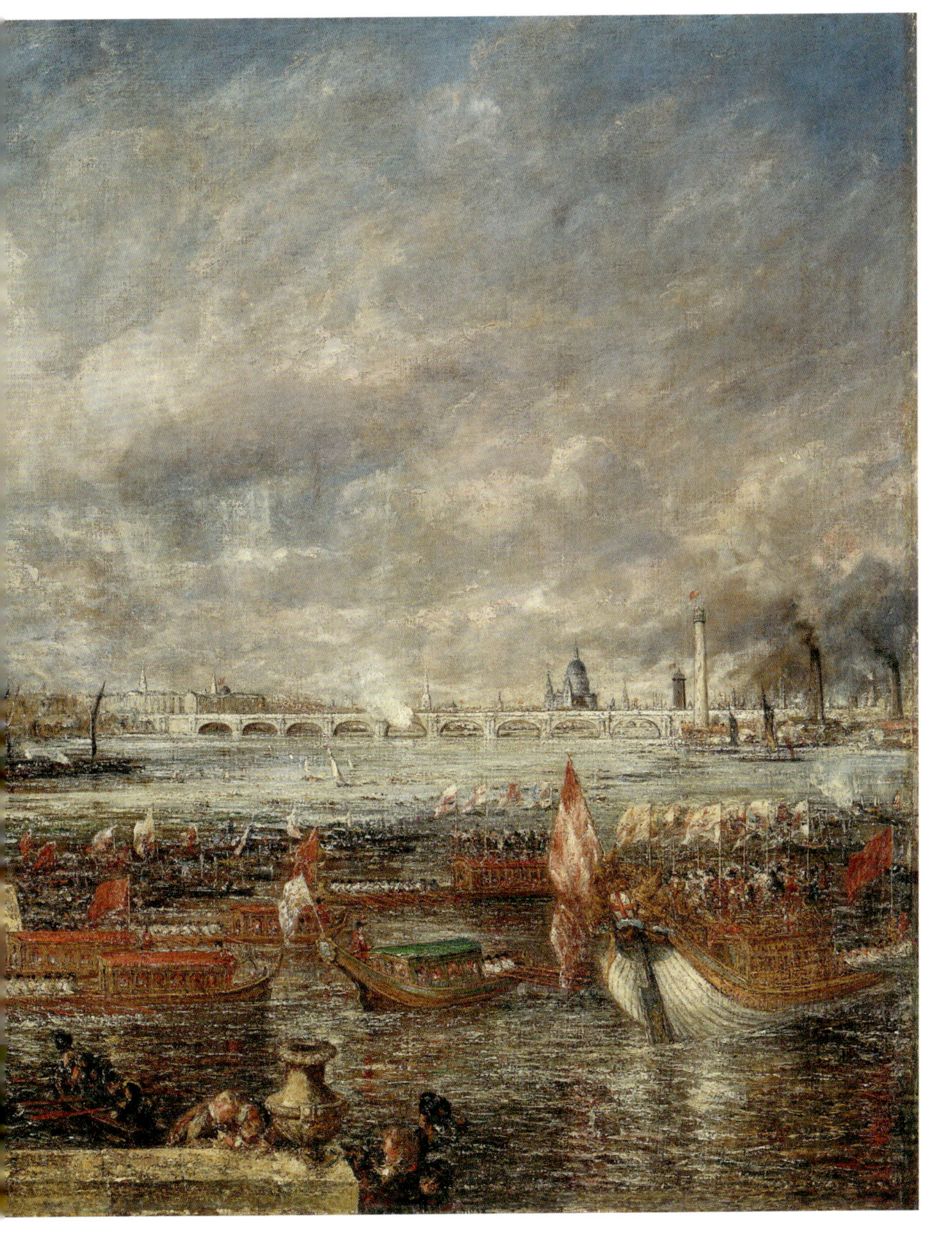

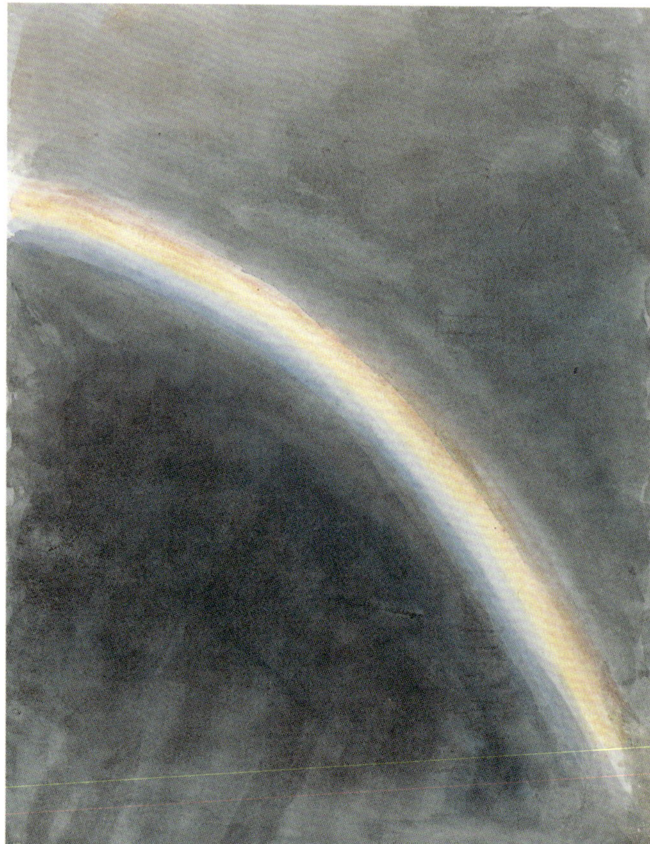

Sky Study with Rainbow 1827
Watercolour on paper
22.5 × 18.4

*London from Hampstead Heath
in a Storm, with a Double
Rainbow* 1831
Watercolour on paper
19.7 × 320

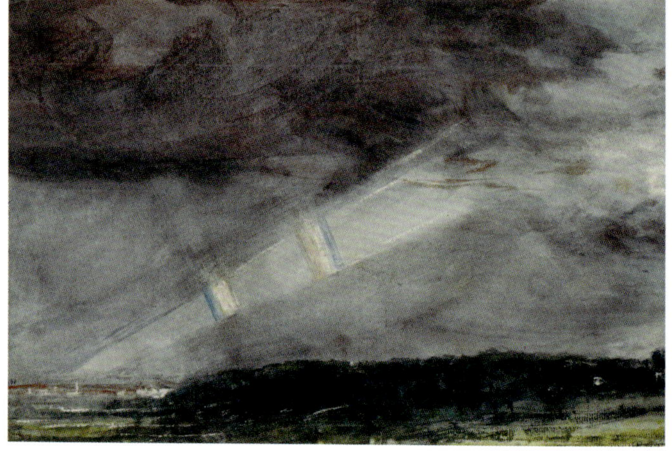

OPPOSITE
Stonehenge 1835,
exh.1836
Pencil and watercolour
on paper
38.7 × 59.1

*The Mound of the City of
Old Sarum from the South*
exh.1834
Watercolour on paper
30.2 × 48.7

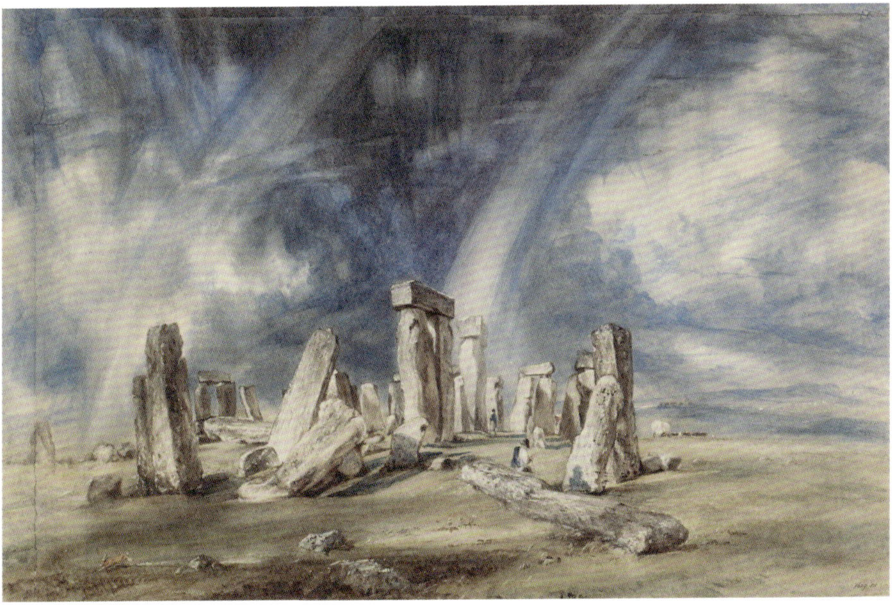

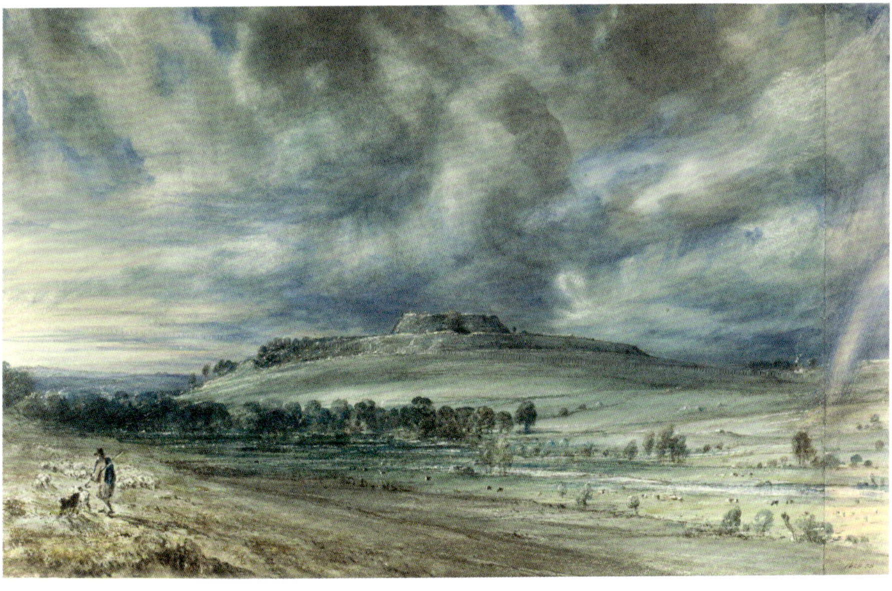

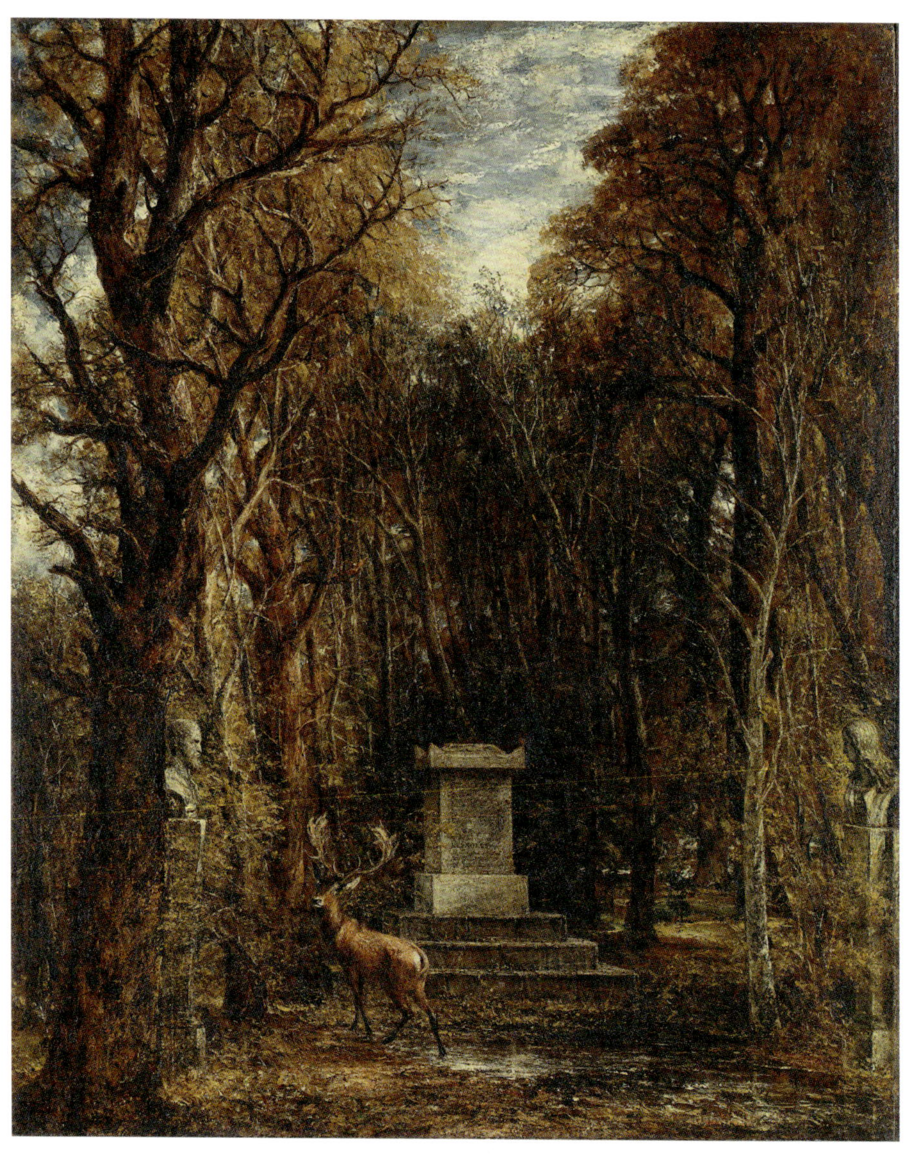

Cenotaph to the Memory of
Sir Joshua Reynolds, erected in
the grounds of Coleorton Hall,
Leicestershire by the late Sir
George Beaumont, Bt. 1833–6
Oil paint on canvas
132 × 108.5

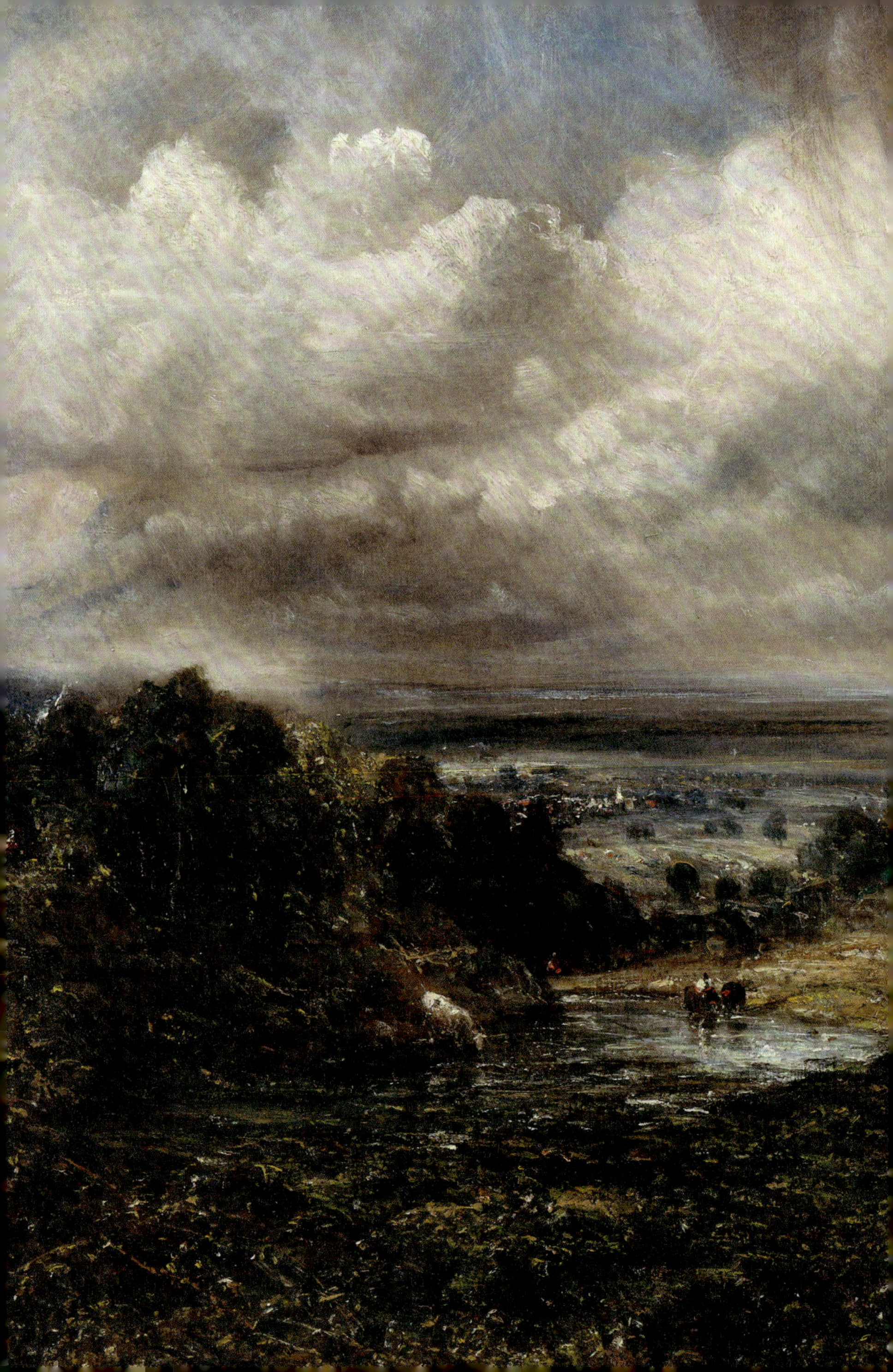

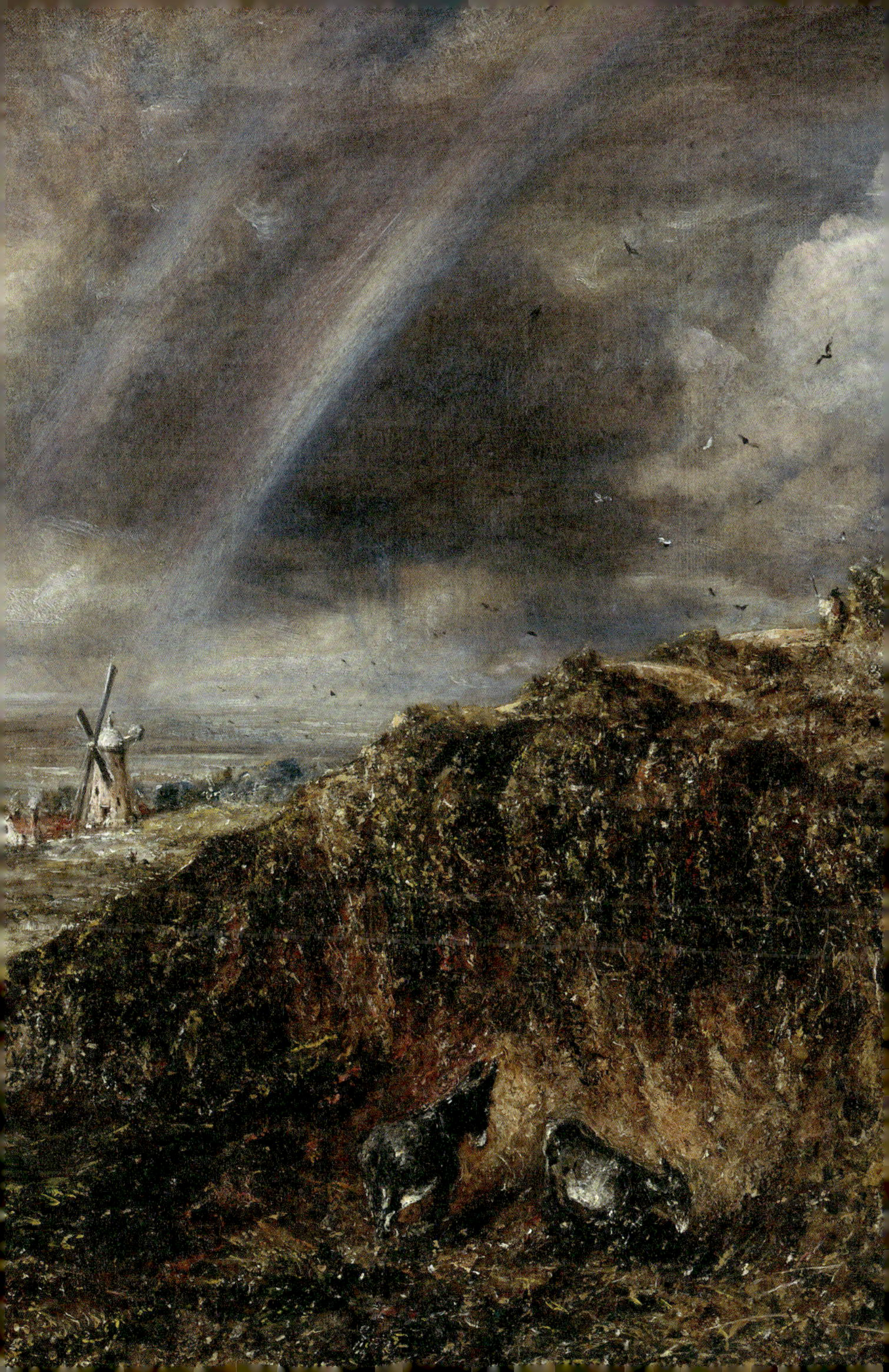

1. C.R. Leslie, *Memoirs of the Life of John Constable, R.A.*, London 1843. For a more recent biography, see Anthony Bailey, *John Constable: A Kingdom of His Own*, London 2006.

2. R.B. Beckett (ed.), *John Constable's Correspondence*, vol.6, Woodbridge 1968, p.82. For Constable and Suffolk, see Emma Roodhouse and Caleb Howgego, *Creating Constable*, Colchester 2021.

3. Joseph Farington, *The Diary of Joseph Farington*, ed. Kathryn Cave, vol.5, London 1982, p.1764a.

4. R.B. Beckett (ed.), *John Constable's Correspondence*, vol.2, Woodbridge 1964, p.32.

5. For portraits, see Martin Gayford and Anne Lyles, *Constable Portraits: The Painter and his Circle*, London 2009.

6. William Gilpin, *Essay on Prints*, London 1768, p.xxi.

7. R.B. Beckett (ed.), *John Constable's Correspondence*, vol.3, Woodbridge 1965, pp.111–12.

8. R.B. Beckett (ed.), *John Constable's Correspondence*, vol.5, Woodbridge 1967, p.882.

9. Leslie 1843, p.316.

10. Beckett (ed.) 1964, p.70.

11. Judy Crosby Ivy, *Constable and the Critics, 1802–1837*, Woodbridge 1991, p.66.

12. Joseph Farington, *The Diary of Joseph Farington*, ed. Kathryn Cave, vol.13, London 1984, p.4564.

13. For a comprehensive survey of the six-footers, see Anne Lyles (ed.), *Constable: The Great Landscapes*, London 2006.

14. The three exceptions were *Chain Pier, Brighton* 1826–7, *Dedham Vale* ?1827–8 and *The Opening of Waterloo Bridge* ('Whitehall Stairs, June 18th, 1817') exh.1832.

15. Beckett (ed.) 1968, p.228.

16. For 'skying', see Nicholas Robbins, 'John Constable, Luke Howard, and the Aesthetics of Climate', *The Art Bulletin*, vol.103, no.2, June 2021, including p.36, no.7.

17. Ivy 1991, pp.133–4.

18. For *England Landscape Scenery*, see Andrew Shirley, *The Published Mezzotints of David Lucas after John Constable, R.A.: A Catalogue and Historical Account*, Oxford 1930.

19. John Barrell, *The Dark Side of the Landscape: The Rural Poor in English Painting 1730–1840*, Cambridge 1980; Michael Rosenthal, *Constable: The Painter and his Landscape*, New Haven and London 1983; Ann Bermingham, *Landscape and Ideology: The English Rustic Tradition, 1740–1860*, London 1987; Andrew Hemingway, *Landscape Imagery and Urban Culture in Early Nineteenth-century Britain*, Cambridge 1992; Stephen Daniels, *Fields of Vision: Landscape Imagery and National Identity in England and the United States*, Cambridge 1993.

20. Beckett (ed.) 1968, p.251. For Constable and Salisbury, see Timothy Wilcox, *Constable and Salisbury: The Soul of Landscape*, Salisbury 2011.

21. 'Subjects and meaning in Salisbury Cathedral from the Meadows', Tate, https://www.tate.org.uk/art/artworks/constable-salisbury-cathedral-from-the-meadows-t13896 in-depth-salisbury-cathedral-from-the-meadows/subjects-meaning, accessed 5 Feb. 2024.

22. For Constable's later years, see Anne Lyles, Matthew Hargraves, Annette Wickham and Mark Pomeroy, *Late Constable*, London 2021.

FURTHER READING

Anthony Bailey, *John Constable: A Kingdom of His Own*, London 2006.

John Barrell, *The Dark Side of the Landscape: The Rural Poor in English Painting 1730–1840*, Cambridge 1980.

R.B. Beckett (ed.), *Constable's Discourses*, Ipswich 1970.

R.B. Beckett (ed.), *John Constable's Correspondence*, 6 vols., Woodbridge 1962–1970. The individual volumes are: vol.1: *The Family at East Bergholt 1807–1837* (1962); vol.2: *Early Friends and Maria Bicknell (Mrs Constable)* (1964); vol.3: *The Correspondence with C.R. Leslie* (1965); vol.4: *Patrons, Dealers and Fellow Artists* (1966); vol.5: *Various Friends with Charles Boner and the Artist's Children* (1967); vol.6: *The Fishers* (1968).

Ann Bermingham, *Landscape and Ideology: The English Rustic Tradition*, London 1987.

Stephen Daniels, *Fields of Vision: Landscape Imagery and National Identity in England and the United States*, Cambridge 1993.

Mark Evans, *John Constable: The Making of a Master*, London 2014.

Joseph Farington, *The Diary of Joseph Farington*, ed. Kathryn Cave, 16 vols., London 1979–85.

Martin Gayford and Anne Lyles, *Constable Portraits: The Painter and his Circle*, London 2009.

William Gilpin, *Essay on Prints*, London 1768 (and later editions).

Andrew Hemingway, *Landscape Imagery and Urban Culture in Early Nineteenth-century Britain*, Cambridge 1992.

Judy Crosby Ivy, *Constable and the Critics, 1802–1837*, Woodbridge 1991.

C.R. Leslie, *Memoirs of the Life of John Constable, R.A.*, London 1843 (and later editions).

Anne Lyles (ed.), *Constable: The Great Landscapes*, London 2006.

Anne Lyles, Matthew Hargraves, Annette Wickham and Mark Pomeroy, *Late Constable*, London 2021.

Leslie Parris and Ian Fleming-Williams, *Constable*, London 1991.

Leslie Parris, Conal Shields and Ian Fleming-Williams, *John Constable: Further Documents and Correspondence*, London and Ipswich 1975.

Graham Reynolds, *The Later Paintings and Drawings of John Constable*, 2 vols., New Haven and London 1984.

Graham Reynolds, *The Early Paintings and Drawings of John Constable*, 2 vols, New Haven and London 1996.

Nicholas Robbins, 'John Constable, Luke Howard, and the Aesthetics of Climate', *The Art Bulletin*, vol.103, no.2, June 2021.

Emma Roodhouse and Caleb Howgego, *Creating Constable*, Colchester 2021.

Michael Rosenthal, *John Constable: The Painter and his Landscape*, New Haven and London 1983.

Andrew Shirley, *The Published Mezzotints of David Lucas after John Constable, R.A.: A Catalogue and Historical Account*, Oxford 1830.

William Vaughan, *John Constable*, London 2002.

Timothy Wilcox, *Constable and Salisbury: The Soul of Landscape*, Salisbury 2011.

CREDITS

First published 2024 by order of the Tate Trustees
by Tate Publishing, a division of Tate Enterprises
Ltd, Millbank, London SW1P 4RG
www.tate.org.uk/publishing

A catalogue record for this book is available from
the British Library

ISBN 978 1 84976 900 6

Distributed in the United States and Canada
by ABRAMS, New York

Library of Congress Control Number applied for

Senior Editor: Emma Poulter
Production: Bill Jones
Picture Researcher: Emma O'Neill
Designed by Astrid Stavro
Colour reproduction by DL Imaging, London
Printed and bound in Italy by Printer Trento S.r.l

Cover: *Salisbury Cathedral from the Meadows* exh.1831
(detail, see pp.80–1)
Frontispiece: *The Hay Wain* 1820–1, exh.1821
(detail, see p.23)

Measurements of artworks are given in
centimetres, height before width and depth

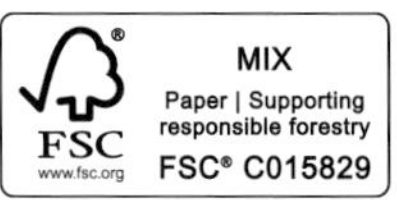

THE AUTHOR
Gillian Forrester is an independent art historian,
curator and writer. She was formerly Senior
Curator of Prints and Drawings at the Yale Center
for British Art and specialises in British print
culture, with a particular focus on John Constable
and J.M.W. Turner.

AUTHOR'S ACKNOWLEDGEMENTS
I am grateful to Guilland Sutherland for her
advice and generous support. Tim Barringer
read and commented on the first draft, making
many helpful suggestions. This book is dedicated
to Anthony Bailey (1933–2020), Constable
biographer, writer, scholar and friend.